Seeking
GOD

Seeking GOD

HOW CHRISTIANITY
MAKES SENSE OF
WHAT A GOD OF
LOVE IS DOING IN
THIS WORLD

Steven L. Skahn

Seeking God

Copyright © 2017 by Steven L. Skahn

All rights reserved.

Published in the United States by Credo House Publishers, a division of Credo Communications, LLC, Grand Rapids, Michigan
credohousepublishers.com

All Scripture quotations, unless otherwise indicated, are taken from the THE HOLY BIBLE, NEW INTERNATIONAL VERSION®, NIV® Copyright © 1973, 1978, 1984 by Biblica, Inc.®. Used by permission. All rights reserved worldwide.

ISBN: 978-1-625860-88-0

Cover and interior design by Frank Gutbrod
Editing by Mike Vander Klipp
Cover image by Pexels.com

Printed in the United States of America
First edition

To Mother
whose many gifts to me have
included her curiosity about all things.

Contents

Preface *1*

1 The Seeming Silence of God *7*

2 The Path to God *23*

3 The Plan of God *43*

4 The Judgment of God *63*

5 The Life God Offers *89*

6 The Knowledge of the Truth about God *113*

Acknowledgments *117*

Preface

When I was a philosophy major at Calvin College, some forty years ago now, the classes raised a question in my mind that I have never been able to shake: Why, of all the possible worlds that God could have created, did he create this one? I was a Christian then, as I am now, and believing Christianity to be true, the question for me has been essentially the question of why is God doing things in the way that Christianity describes. It is also the question of why is God doing things in the way we see taking place in the events in the world around us—both throughout history and in the day to day events of our lives.

As I have talked to friends who are not Christians, as I have seen the arguments set forth in our culture against Christianity, and as I have read and studied the Bible, the question has always been there. If God is as Christianity describes him, then he is a God of love. If he is a loving God, then he certainly is fair. But if Christianity is true, and if God is really calling on all people to repent and accept Jesus as their savior, how can this be fair when Christianity seems so implausible to so many, and when there are so many competing religions in the world.

Over the years answers have slowly come that have, at least, been helpful to me. These answers have allowed me to rest in the belief that the love of God really is the driving force behind everything taking place in this world. They are answers that would have been helpful to me as a young man. They are also answers that I believe may be helpful to others. They provide the basis for this book.

This book is written as a case for the Christian faith. The first chapter, entitled The Seeming Silence of God, asks why God, assuming he exists, does not make crystal clear who he is by, for example, interrupting our television coverage or the internet to declare himself. It concludes with the suggestion that God may want us to seek him, and suggests some reasons why that might be the case.

The second chapter, entitled The Path to God, asks how—if we are going to seek God—do we go about it. Starting with a consideration of the role of love in our lives, it argues that if we really do earnestly seek God, and in doing so, seek to love God and love those around us, we are going to discover we have a need that can only be met in Jesus Christ.

The third chapter, entitled The Plan of God, considers the possibility that Christianity is true, and asks if it makes sense. This chapter deals most directly with the earlier-asked question of why, of all the possible worlds that God could have created, he created this one. The argument is made that in order for God to accomplish what he ultimately is going to accomplish—a paradise where all who love him will live with him forever—it was likely necessary for him to have allowed us to experience in our lives both love and selfishness.

By our experience of both, two results have followed. First, as we all see the joy that comes from love, we each have a decision to make about how we feel about its opposite, selfishness. Are we OK with the selfishness in our lives, or do we see it as something for which we need God's forgiveness? Second, for all who do seek God's forgiveness, when God brings us to the paradise he is going to create, our memory of the pain and destruction caused by selfishness will likely play a crucial role in allowing us to never be tempted by it again. Not being tempted by selfishness, we will be free to always and only love God and love each other.

The fourth chapter, entitled The Judgment of God, deals with the most difficult part of Christian belief: the idea that God will judge the world. Jesus taught "repent or you will all perish." How is this fair? How is this consistent with God being a God of love? This chapter argues that it is consistent with God being a God of love for God to hate selfishness. And if we, throughout the entirety of our lives, never repent of our selfishness, have we not embraced this thing that God hates? God's judgment will be fair because it will be based on the moral judgments we have made of other people. By these judgments we have all shown that we know right and wrong. We have all condemned in others things that we have done ourselves. Knowing this, we have no excuse for not repenting of the wrong we have done.

The fifth chapter, entitled The Life God Offers, looks at the Christian life, asking if it is something one would expect from a good and loving God. It seeks to show that God's relationship with the Christian is just what one would expect from such a God.

The very brief sixth chapter, Knowing the Truth About God, acknowledges that this book does not purport to have proven that Christianity is true. It has only sought to establish that Christianity offers a plausible explanation for how a God of love could be responsible for this world. As to whether Christianity is actually true, this is not going to be established by argument. God is not looking for smart people who can understand complex arguments. God is rather looking for people with contrite hearts who see they need a Savior. Such people, assuming Christianity is true, will discover it is true by the work of God in their hearts after they accept Christ as their Savoir.

CHAPTER 1

The Seeming Silence of God

When God, assuming he exists, created this world, how did he go about it? When we, in our lives, take on a project of some sort, we will first have a goal in mind. We will then devise a plan by which to accomplish the goal. Then, if we believe that the goal is worth the effort and the plan has a reasonably good chance of success, we will execute the plan.

In creating this world and this universe, did God act in a similar way? It is hard to imagine that he did not. It is hard to imagine that he would have created this universe without a clear goal in mind and a precise plan by which he could accomplish that goal. But if so—again assuming God exists—what was the goal, and what was the plan? How does the plan explain the events that we see transpiring around us—and that have been happening throughout the history of this world?

Of course it could be that God does not exist. It could be that all that is happening around us, and all that has happened since the Big Bang, is happening by random chance in a godless universe. While this is possible, most of us do not believe it. While the tenets of atheism could be true, most of us are not atheists. We may be mistaken, but most of us believe that God exists. We have a sense that there is a God who is responsible for this world and who is responsible for our existence. Whether God created us directly or acted through evolutionary processes, most of us believe that we are not the result of an accident.

The atheist would claim that this is naïve simplicity—that no one can reasonably believe that a god, and certainly not a good god, could have created a world in which there is so much pain and suffering. But let us consider whether that is necessarily so. Let us consider whether a good God might have had a goal in all of this—one that would be worthy of him—that might help us make sense of what is happening in this world.

Can We Ask the Question? Should We?

However, to ask such questions—what God's goal might be and how the events of this world might be accomplishing it—undoubtedly strikes many of us as asking things that are unknowable. Although these would certainly be among the most important questions that we could ever ask, they are questions we usually tend to avoid. Most of us have our own personal beliefs about God; however, they are just that: our own personal beliefs. Our beliefs about God are, for most of us, comforting. But most of us are not so certain of our beliefs that we would declare them to be true in any objective sense. To try to go beyond this—beyond holding simply personal beliefs about God—to try to find answers that would truly describe what God is actually doing in this world beyond our own personal opinions, would be to engage in an effort that most of us would consider useless.

As we approach the subject of God's purposes in the world, we might consider whether asking such questions is useless because, really, how could a person come to know the truth about God? There are untold numbers of religions in the world that say, or seem to say, different things about God. In such a pluralistic atmosphere, how could any of us objectively come to know which, if any, of these teachings or religions accurately describe God? Maybe they all provide paths to the same God. How would it be possible for any one person to determine that any one religion is actually true, in contrast to other religions, which are false? If we did start to think that we had discovered the one "true" religion, we at that point would be on dangerous ground—ground on which many arrogant people have stood as they have used their religious beliefs to justify intolerant and even violent behavior. The history of the world is full of holy wars and terrorist acts conducted by people who were certain that they knew and were carrying out God's will.

As a result, we tend not to bother asking what would otherwise seem to be the most important questions we could ever ask. Important as these questions may be, thinking about them would seem to be a waste of time. If we did think about them and started to believe that we were arriving at answers, we would likely become worse for the effort—more arrogant and intolerant than what we were at the outset. Pondering who God actually is and what he might be doing in the world seems to be, therefore, a no-win proposition.

A God Who Allows the Tension

Now what is especially intriguing is the thought that if God does exist, and if what is happening in this world is happening according to his plan, then as part of his plan he has allowed this state of affairs to exist. He has allowed it to seem a waste of time, at best, and dangerous, at worst, to consider who he is or what he is about. And so he has allowed many or most of us to live lives in which we, for all intents and purposes, ignore him. He even allows us to deny that he exists. Whether we deny he exists or whether we believe that he probably does exist but pay little attention to him, we can quite comfortably live our lives without blatantly obvious adverse effects. One thing is clear: God is not strong-arming us into paying attention to him. He is not nagging us either.

This raises the question why. If God exists, why would he not force us to pay attention to him? And if he has a plan that he is carrying out in this world, why isn't he announcing it in a way that we all could easily and obviously recognize it and thereby know just what he expects from us? Why, in contrast, would he allow it to seem so useless to ask who he is and what he may be doing in this world?

Why does God Seem to Be Silent?

As mentioned above, one possible answer, of course, is that he does not exist. If there is no God, then there is no plan. And a God who is not there cannot be nagging us to believe in him. But since most people in the world are not atheists, let us consider whether there is any other possibility. Let us consider the possibility that while God exists, he has nevertheless, as part of his plan, allowed his existence to be a matter that can be debated.

Since we have the ability to speak and communicate, it would be reasonable to believe that God could also, in one way or another, speak. One would certainly expect that if God made us, either directly or through guiding evolutionary processes, that he would have the capacity to do anything that we can do. But if he can speak, why doesn't he? Why does he not tell us why he made us and what, if anything, he wants from us?

Different religions, of course, claim that God *has* spoken. They claim that he has revealed himself through their prophets or religious teachers who have recorded these revelations in their revered writings. But if God has spoken through any or all of these religions, why is he not telling us that today? He could easily, it would seem, interrupt our television coverage to point us in the right direction.

Possibly the reason God is not announcing himself to us in some dramatic fashion is because he does not care about us. Perhaps he made us solely for his own entertainment. Maybe he enjoys watching us muddle through our lives. If so, he may find it amusing to hear what all the different religions have to say about him. However, this seems unlikely. If such were the case, it would be like a parent giving birth to a child, only to later care nothing for the child and use him or her only as a source of amusement. We know how we would feel about a parent who acted in this way. It would be contemptible. In the same way, if God acted in this way towards us, it would strike us as dishonorable on his part.

But if God intended that we exist and caused us to be the way we are, then perhaps it is precisely because of him that we can formulate this kind of a judgment—the judgment that it would have been wrong for God to have made us just for his amusement. And if God has made us in such a way that we would condemn a god who would make us and not care about us, it is at least possible, if not likely, that God would also hate such a god. It could be that it would be as unthinkable for God to act this way towards us as it would be for most parents to act this way towards their children.

Considering these possibilities does not, of course, prove anything about God. Maybe he is out to trick us; maybe he is uncaring or even malicious. But just as we would not want to believe that our parents do not care or are malicious towards us, it may be more than coincidence that we tend not to want to believe these things about God. Consider how strange it would be, if God really was uncaring and malicious, that he would have made us in such a way that we would see his actions as dishonorable. Instead, it would seem more likely—and even more reasonable—that God has enabled us to make these kinds of moral judgments because he is a morally good God who does not do dishonorable things. Let us at least consider this possibility.

Why would a *Good* God Seem to Be Silent?

If God is morally good, the question then becomes: is there any reason why a good God who cares about us would not be speaking up in such a way that none of us could deny who he is or what, if anything, he wants from us?

One possible answer to this question is that while God cares about us, he does not want anything from us. Perhaps he also does not care what we think of him. It could be that he created us with no other plan than that we might just enjoy what we could of our lives for as long as we live, and then simply die. If God does not care what we think of him, then he certainly would not care what religion we adopt while we were living our lives here on earth—if we choose to adopt any at all. And if his overarching goal was simply that we enjoy ourselves as best we can, then it would seem that his only concern would be that we not adopt intolerant religious views that would interfere with other people's enjoyment of life.

This possibility fits nicely with contemporary views. We tend to believe that it does not matter what religion a person believes in, as long as he or she is sincere on the one hand, and is at least tolerant of differing religious beliefs on the other hand. These commonly held views of religion would be entirely correct if God does not care about religion. They would be entirely sensible if God made us for no other reason than that we might enjoy our lives as best we can for as long as we are alive.

If we stop, however, to ask if this makes sense, some questions arise. If God made us for no other purpose than that we might enjoy, as best we can, our lives here on earth, we might ask, couldn't he have done a better job? While there is much to enjoy in this world, there is also, and undeniably, much pain. Could not God have made things a little more enjoyable and a lot less painful? And if his plan was nothing other than that we might enjoy ourselves in this world, why would he have made us finite creatures? In other words, why do we have to die? Why not just let us go on enjoying ourselves forever? Unless God's power is limited and this is the best he is able to do, one might think that he could have made us so that we could carry on indefinitely, getting what pleasure we could from our lives.

And if God really does not care about religion, then again, why be silent? Why not speak up and tell us this? This kind of information would surely be helpful. He could have saved the people of this world from endless conflict, heartache, contention, and even death and warfare by making this clear. If God exists, and if he cares about us and if this is his view on religion, why not just say so?

At this point we might be tempted to throw up our hands, believing we have just confirmed what was suggested earlier in the chapter—that it is useless to ask these questions. Or we might go back and conclude that we were in fact deluding ourselves when we theorized that God exists or that he is good. But first let us ask whether we have exhausted all of the possible conclusions. Is there any other possible reason why a good God who cares about us would not speak out in a way that no one could deny who he is and what he what he wants from us?

A Possible Answer: God Wants Us to Seek Him

There is another possibility. Perhaps God wants us to seek him.

We certainly have reasons why we might want to seek him. There are many wonderful things that we experience in our lives that would warrant, if God exists, giving him our thanks and our praise. At times, we are almost overwhelmed by wonder—such as when we have a clear view of the Milky Way, or when we first hold a newborn child, or when we fall in love. In such moments, when we are staggered by what we are experiencing, it seems natural to think about God—to wonder if there is someone there to whom we owe thanks. It may be that God wants us to ask that question—whether he exists. And perhaps he not only wants us to ask it, but also to attempt to answer it.

Additionally, we all face trouble in our lives. At times our troubles seem overwhelming. In the midst of such moments, it again seems natural to think of God—to wonder if he exists and if can help us. Again, perhaps these are exactly the questions that God wants us to ask.

If this is true—that God wants us to seek him and has given us reasons to do so—then it may be that God has also made it possible for us to find him. Maybe if we would only seek him, we would not only find that he exists, but also discover who he is.

Of course, as discussed above, this seems preposterous. How could it be so simple? So all we need to do is seek God and we will find him? Something in our gut tells us this cannot be. It completely goes against everything that the culture we live in tells us. Nevertheless, as impossible as it seems, let us at least consider the possibility that it is true.

In the next chapter we will do just that: we will consider whether it is possible to find God if we will only seek him.

Putting that question aside for the moment, let us here ask another question: why might God want us to seek him? As noted above, if God exists, it would seem to be a simple thing for him to interrupt our television coverage, or take control of the internet, to announce that he exists, and to tell us who he is. Why instead of that, would he prefer that we seek him?

If God exists, and if he has created this world, as well as the amazing universe it is a part of, he must be great indeed—greater than anything we can imagine. If then this great God has given us reasons to seek him—such as to thank him for the wonders we experience in life, or to seek his help when we seem to be drowning amidst its difficulties—and we nevertheless decide we are not going to be bothered to do so, maybe God is willing to let us live with that choice. This would make sense if God is looking for relationships with those who want to know him and choose to seek him. For those who do not, it may be beneath his dignity to beg them to pay attention to him.

Certainly, this would be consistent with the way we live our lives. If we are interested in getting to know someone, whether as a friend or a lover, we will show that person our kindness and attention. If we then invite the person to do something, and he or she responds in such a way that makes clear that he or she has no interest in getting together, then we generally do best to discontinue, or at least lessen, our efforts to establish a relationship. We might, for a time, wait for the person to have a change of heart, but we diminish ourselves if we essentially start begging the person for his or her attention. Alternatively, if we start pursing the person more and more aggressively, we eventually become stalkers. Neither begging nor stalking seems to be a good way to start a relationship.

If it is beneath our dignity to pursue relationships in such ways, it makes sense that it is beneath God's as well. By creating us, and by giving us so many things to enjoy in life, God may believe that he has made crystal clear how much he cares for us. Having done so, he has given us strong reasons to seek him. And if he has also made it possible for us to find him, then if we do not seek him, the onus is on us. If we have the opportunity to seek out and know God, and we do not know God, then it is because we do not care to know him.

What Jesus Taught About Our Finding God.

It is interesting to note that this possibility—that God wants us to seek him—is what Jesus believed. He said:

> Enter through the narrow gate. For wide is the gate and broad is the road that leads to destruction, and many enter through it. But small is the gate and narrow the road that leads to life, and only a few find it. (Matthew 7:13-14)

In Jesus' view, there is a narrow gate that we need to find. If we stay on what he calls the broad road and do not look for the narrow gate, we will miss it. But the narrow gate, he seems to imply, is right there. If we look for it, we will see it.

Let us consider Jesus' statement as a hypothesis to consider. He believes that God wants us to seek him. Let us not assume that he is correct. Rather, let us ask if this could make sense.

Jesus' statement raises obvious questions, not the least of which would be, how could it be so simple? With all of the religions in the world, how is anyone going to find this narrow gate? And what can he mean by saying the broad road leads to destruction? If God is good, how can he condemn anyone for not finding the right gate, let alone a narrow gate?

These are all questions to consider, but to begin, let us start with these: First, does Jesus give us any explanation for his confidence that we can find this narrow gate? Second, does he say anything that might explain why God would seem to remain silent while so many are missing the gate, headed down the broad road that he says leads to destruction?

Jesus' statement regarding the broad and narrow gates comes from the Sermon on the Mount. In this sermon Jesus explains, if not how we find the narrow gate, at least why he is sure that if we look for it we will find it. He says:

> Ask and it will be given to you; seek and you will find; knock and the door will be opened to you. For everyone who asks receives; the one who seeks finds; and to the one who knocks, the door will be opened.
>
> Which of you, if his son asks for bread, will give him a stone? Or if he asks for a fish, will give

him a snake? If you, then, though you are evil, know how to give good gifts to your children, how much more will your Father in heaven give good gifts to those who ask him! (Matthew 7:7-11)

Jesus believed that anyone can find the narrow gate. All we need to do is ask God. God will not deny us. He will show us. For Jesus it was inconceivable that if we genuinely desired to find God, we would not be able to do so.

Now it is striking how different Jesus' view is from our view. We do not seek God, because it seems utterly useless to think we can find him. Jesus believed that it was not useless to try to find God. He believed that those who seek him will certainly find him. Either Jesus was speaking nonsense, or there is something right in front of our faces that we are missing.

But even if this is the case—that the narrow gate is right there for us to see—why would God let people walk by? Why hasn't he closed off the broad road, forcing everyone through the narrow gate? A possibility arises from another teaching of Jesus. He told us:

> Do not give dogs what is sacred; do not throw your pearls to the pigs. If you do, they may trample them under their feet, and then turn and tear you to pieces. (Matthew 7:6)

In teaching this, Jesus may have given us an insight into the way God treats us. It may be that what lies behind the narrow gate are the treasures that are most sacred to God. Perhaps he knows that many or even most of us would have no use for those treasures. Upon discovering them, we might simply trample them under our feet.

Others of us, however, might sense that something is missing on the broad road. We might start looking for something we are not finding there. For those who do start looking, the narrow gate—from what Jesus tells us—is right there. Going to it, we may see beyond it a road full of the treasures for which we long.

On the broad road, however, many of us tend to be busy with everything that that road offers. We do not notice and do not care that something is missing. We do not stop to look for anything other than what we find right in front us as we walk along the road. Distracted, we do not see the narrow gate. We walk right by.

Perhaps God has a plan in which he needs to separate those of us who share his view of what is most precious in life from those of us who do not. And maybe all of us who share his view of what is most precious will look for it. Seeking the narrow gate, we will find it.

CHAPTER 2

The Path to God

Let us consider the possibility that God exists, that he wants us to seek him—and not only to seek him, but to find him. To use the picture that Jesus used, let us consider the possibility that somewhere in plain view there is a narrow gate that leads to God. But where? Why aren't we seeing it? Where should we be looking?

If Jesus is right, and if God wants and expects us to find this gate, then the means of finding it must seemingly relate to important things in our lives. Indeed, if this is the most important issue of our lives—whether we seek and find God—then we might expect that the most important things in our lives will point us in the right direction.

This makes sense if God wants us to find him. We would not expect that the path to God would be found in trivial and unimportant things. Trivial and unimportant things are things we can rightly ignore. If God does not want us to ignore him, then the path to him would have to be found in something that we cannot ignore. The path to him must be found in something we each, in our individual lives, must confront. There must be an issue so important and so common to humanity that every individual will at some point in their lives have to deal with it—that's where we'll find the narrow gate.

So let us start by looking at the big picture of our lives. What in our lives is most important? What gives our lives meaning? If there is a way to find God, it must, it would seem, relate to this.

Love

For many, if not most of us, the answer is obvious: Love gives our lives meaning. While there may be lots of things that are important to us, and lots of things on which we are focused, there is nothing that enriches our lives as much as the love and kindness that we share with family and friends.

This has been true from the time our lives began. When we came into this world as infants, nothing was more important than that we were loved by our parents. If we grew up in an environment where we experienced lots of love, we benefited greatly—both in our happiness then and in our developing a sense of well-being that would assist us through the rest of our lives. If we grew up in an environment where we experienced little love, we suffered—both then and into our adult lives.

As infants we were powerless to take care of our own needs. Although we had nothing tangible to offer our parents, most of us experienced their love. For most parents, the wonder of a newborn baby compels them to watch over it almost constantly; to watch, to wonder, to worry, to care for and provide for it. Usually, they almost compulsively put the child's interests before their own. And in doing so, in taking care of the child, in sacrificing their interests for the child's welfare, they normally experience a joy and a happiness that causes them to continue what they have begun—caring for the child as the child grows. And through that relationship, both parent and child learn something important about the beauty of what love is.

As we grow older, we experience love in a powerful but different way when we ourselves meet another person and fall in love. When this happens we are, for at least a time, overwhelmed by our feelings for another person. We want to do anything we can for that person. Almost in spite of ourselves, we strongly desire to make sacrifices for the benefit of the one we love.

It would seem that this is the essence of love—to put another person's interests before our own. Most of us probably feel that we are at our best when we do this: when we give of ourselves for the sake of another.

Part of the wonder of giving or receiving love is that no one is actually compelled to do it. We may have strong emotional reasons to put another's interests first—such as a parent's love for a child, or when we fall in love—but the actual decision to do it is voluntary. When we do make the choice to put the good of another person before our own, it usually feels right. It is good for us and good for the person we love.

In greater and lesser ways, we continually see people doing this. It obviously can happen in any kind of relationship. Sometimes it simply involves kindness or good manners: opening the door for someone, letting another driver merge into our lane, or giving money to someone in need. At other times it is heroic: diving into the lake to save someone who is drowning, or rushing into a burning building to carry a disabled person to safety. In any context when a person genuinely appears to be putting another's person's interests first, we appreciate it. If we are the recipient of that kindness, we are grateful.

Selfishness

We know how special love is, in part, because we know its opposite. We know what it is like when people decide to put themselves before others. Parents may neglect a child's needs in order to pursue their own career or other interests. A husband or wife may decide to put work or some other activity—such as a sport, or a hobby, or devoting an undue amount of attention to social media—before the well-being of his or her spouse. In contrast to love, which tends to bring people closer together, selfishness drives people apart.

Just as love can cover a broad range of things, from simple acts of kindness to acts of heroism, so selfishness exists on a continuum, ranging from thoughtlessness or rudeness to vicious acts of violence. Whereas love usually benefits another person, selfishness causes harm.

Just as we applaud and praise those who make sacrifices for the good of others, so we also criticize and condemn those who act in their own interests to the harm of others. We cannot help being affected by selfish behavior—whether it is someone being rude or disrespectful, or someone acting viciously, we react negatively. As a society, if a person's selfish behavior crosses certain lines, we consider it criminal, and put that person in jail. As individuals, when we see a person acting selfishly to the harm of another, we judge them. Whether we confront the person or speak of it to others, we at least in our minds make a negative judgment about what the person has done. Just as something in us responds positively to individuals who make sacrifices for others, so also something in us responds negatively when we see individuals putting their own desires before the well-being of others.

We are speaking of things that are obvious, but the pervasiveness of these dynamics may escape us. It isn't just a matter of the ways individuals interact with each other; persistent selfishness may also pervade groups, organizations and governments. When one group acts selfishly to the harm of another, we condemn it. It can obviously happen in all sorts of ways: one racial group mistreats another; a government oppresses its citizens; a corporation puts its profits ahead of the harm it may be doing to people or the environment. Whenever we perceive individuals or institutions trampling others' rights, we condemn it and desire that justice somehow be done.

Our response to selfish behavior is often anger. Most of the anger we experience in life is due to what we perceive to be selfishness. It tends to arise spontaneously in us when we see one person hurting another. We most often get angry when we are the ones who are getting injured. Sometimes our anger is appropriate to the circumstances; at other times we become enraged about trivial matters. But whether our anger is appropriate or wildly excessive, it is normally fueled by what we perceive to be one person selfishly disregarding the interests of ourselves or others.

Is there any dynamic more important in our lives than this dynamic between love and selfishness? We have many activities and goals in our lives, but nothing touches us more deeply than this. We are continually seeing and feeling the goodness of love and kindness on the one hand, and the ugliness of selfishness on the other.

Now if God exists, and if he has a plan that is being carried out in this world, then it would seem that his plan must relate to this dynamic. He certainly has made us in such a way that we cannot help but long for love. We also cannot help but hate selfishness. Everything that is going on around us every day is highlighting these truths: love and kindness are constructive to our lives; selfishness is destructive. If part of God's plan was to make these truths evident, he could not have done a better job.

But where does this lead us? Is there in the midst of these truths something that could lead us to God?

Looking At Ourselves

Well, one thing we can do is take the eyes with which we look at everyone around us and turn them on ourselves. What do we see? We see that we too are selfish. We are full of this thing that we condemn in others. All of us, in ways large and small, put our interests before the interests of others. Sometimes we hurt or belittle others. Sometimes we see those around us with needs that we could meet, and we decide not to meet them. We would rather please ourselves. When we see selfishness in others, we get angry. When we see it in ourselves, what do we do?

One thing we could do is ignore it. Even though we take the selfishness of others very seriously, we could excuse it in ourselves. When we put our own interests before the interests of others we always have reasons for doing it. We could be perfectly satisfied by our reasons. Or we could just accept that this is the way life is. We could decide it is no big deal, that nobody is perfect, and that it is nothing to get excited about. We could look at all of the good things that we have done and decide that, on balance, we are not so bad. We could also look at the selfishness of others, and see it as the basis for reassurance—it shows that our selfishness is not unusual. It is entirely common. We are not any worse than others. We are better than most.

Another option would be to neither ignore it nor accept it. We could realize that the selfishness of our lives is inexcusable. Maybe we have an excuse for this act of unkindness or that lack of generosity, but for the vast majority of it, there is no good excuse. We could see that the way to live is to love, and that over and over again we have failed to do so. In seeing this, we could see that just as we condemn others when they are selfish, so we also deserve condemnation for our own selfishness. In fact, we could conclude that maybe we deserve God's condemnation.

But if we come to this latter conclusion, what should we do? When we hurt another person we know what we should do. We should go and say we are sorry. That is the road to beginning to repair the damage we have done. This is certainly needed when we offend others, but is this something that we should also be saying to God? Most of us believe God exists. If we see that we have acted in ways that deserve God's condemnation, should we not then seek God's mercy? We could ask him for forgiveness. We do not have to know much about God in order to call out to him in repentance for the selfishness of our lives.

Is it possible that everything going on around us is designed to get us to this point—to the point that we see that the selfishness in our lives is not some trivial thing that we can just ignore? We do not ignore it in others. Should we ignore it in ourselves? God has given us life in a world in which the goodness of love is evident. When we see that we have often not loved those around us, should we stay silent towards God? Might the path to God be found in seeking his forgiveness?

But We Lack Feelings of Remorse

Nevertheless, for most of us, this is unrealistic. We do not feel any need to seek God's forgiveness. When we have hurt a person whom we care about, we feel bad about it. We want to go to them and say we are sorry. But we do not feel that way about God; we do not feel any need to tell him that we are sorry. While we all have to admit that we have done things that are wrong, and occasionally our consciences make us squirm, most of the time we do not feel any great distress. We basically feel fine about ourselves. After all, there is more good in our lives than bad. We can live with ourselves. We can usually sleep at night. We do not feel a need to come to God in repentance.

But maybe we should stop for a minute and consider whether our self-reassuring feelings might be misleading us. In light of some of the basic concepts we have been considering, there is reason why we should consider this possibility. As we have noted, most of us believe that God exists. If we are correct, and he does exist, then it seems that he has made us in a way that we, on the one hand, long for love, and on the other hand, hate selfishness. A reasonable explanation for why God might have made us this way is that God also loves love and hates selfishness. But if these things are true we can see, at least theoretically, that God would have reason to be angry with us. We are often selfish. If God does have reason to be angry with us, then even though we don't feel it, maybe we should feel a need to repent. Maybe there is something wrong with our feelings.

But what could be wrong? Why would our feelings mislead us? Two conversations that Jesus had suggest a possibility.

How Jesus Addressed the Self-Satisfied

An expert in Jewish law once asked Jesus, "What must I do to inherit eternal life?" (Luke 10:25). On other occasions Jesus had taught, "[U]nless you repent, you too will all perish." (Luke 13:3). But on this occasion he did not answer the man this way. Rather, Jesus responded with a question, asking the man how he read the law on this issue. The expert answered:

> "'Love the Lord your God with all your heart and with all your soul and with all your strength and with all your mind'; and 'Love your neighbor as yourself.'" (Luke 10:27)

The discussion continued as follows:

> "You have answered correctly," Jesus replied. "Do this and you will live."
>
> But he wanted to justify himself, so he asked Jesus, "And who is my neighbor?"

In reply Jesus said: "A man was going down from Jerusalem to Jericho, when he was attacked by robbers. They stripped him of his clothes, beat him and went away, leaving him half dead. A priest happened to be going down the same road, and when he saw the man, he passed by on the other side. So too, a Levite, when he came to the place and saw him, passed by on the other side. But a Samaritan, as he traveled, came where the man was; and when he saw him, he took pity on him. He went to him and bandaged his wounds, pouring on oil and wine. Then he put the man on his own donkey, took him to an inn and took care of him. The next day he took out two denarii and gave them to the innkeeper. 'Look after him,' he said, 'and when I return, I will reimburse you for any extra expense you may have.'"

"Which of these three do you think was a neighbor to the man who fell into the hands of robbers?"

The expert in the law replied, "The one who had mercy on him."

Jesus told him, "Go and do likewise." (Luke 10:28-37)

Jesus told the man to live like the Good Samaritan and he would obtain eternal life. Was Jesus being inconsistent—on the one hand telling some to repent, and on the other hand telling this man he would be saved if he lived like the Good Samaritan?

Another man also approached Jesus with the same question: "Teacher, what good thing must I do to get eternal life?" (Matthew 19:16). Jesus responded:

> "Why do you ask me about what is good?" Jesus replied. "There is only One who is good. If you want to enter life, keep the commandments."
>
> "Which ones?" he inquired.
>
> Jesus replied, "'You shall not murder, you shall not commit adultery, you shall not steal, you shall not give false testimony, honor your father and mother,' and 'love your neighbor as yourself.'"
>
> "All these I have kept," the young man said. "What do I still lack?"
>
> Jesus answered, "If you want to be perfect, go, sell your possessions and give to the poor, and you will have treasure in heaven. Then come, follow me."
>
> When the young man heard this, he went away sad, because he had great wealth. (Matthew 19:16-22)

Again Jesus did not tell the man to repent, but rather to sell his possessions and to come follow him. Was Jesus being inconsistent in telling this man that he could obtain eternal life by selling his possessions?

Discovering Sin

Jesus was not being inconsistent if he was striving to lead each of these men to a point where they would feel truly repentant. If he had simply told them to repent, these men—each of whom felt they were doing pretty well in obeying the law—would not have known from what they would need to repent. Each of these men obviously cared about God and about the Jewish law. But they each seemed to believe that they could be saved by obeying the law. Jesus did not directly contradict them; rather, he showed them what the Jewish law really required of them. He taught them what it really means to love God and to love their neighbor as themselves. He told the rich man that he needed to love God more than his money. He told the expert in the law that he needed to love others as the Good Samaritan did. Jesus was leading them to a point of discovery: the discovery that they were not able to live the lives that God required of them. The rich man, who went away sad, was either unwilling or emotionally unable to do what Jesus had asked. If the expert in the law had listened to Jesus and set his heart on living like the Good Samaritan he might, with extraordinary effort, have been able to live like this for a day or two. But to live like this day in and day out, treating all his injured neighbors in this way, was more than he—or any of us—could do.

Many, if not most, of us use our conscience in a way similar to the way these Jewish men used their law. We look at the good things we do and feel pretty good about ourselves. But perhaps our conscience should be leading us in a different direction. We must acknowledge that despite whatever good things we do, there is a dark and pervasive streak of selfishness in our lives. What would happen if we set our hearts on trying to get rid of all of it? What if we began trying, day after day, to live like the Good Samaritan? What if we set our hearts on striving to always love our neighbors in ways that included being willing to use our money for their benefit?

If we genuinely began trying to live like this, we too would make a discovery—the same discovery that Jesus was pointing his questioners toward. It's the same discovery that the Apostle Paul made: When he tried to please God, he discovered that something was stopping him. He wrote:

> For I have the desire to do what is good, but I cannot carry it out. For what I do is not the good

Finding The Solution For Our Sin

If Jesus was right about the broad road and the narrow gate, then Paul's question, "Who will save me?" gets us looking for the narrow gate. We are looking for a way to get rid of the sin that prevents us from pleasing God. We are looking for peace with God. We see that nothing on the broad road can give us relief from the misery we are feeling. And we see that no one else on that road shares our misery. Those we meet on that road may feel their conscience squirm about one thing or another, or feel regrets about certain things they have done. But those feelings are very different from longing to please God and coming to the realization that we cannot. When we realize that we cannot please God, we know we deserve God's condemnation. Knowing this, we feel afraid.

A line in the hymn *Amazing Grace* captures this moment in a person's life: "'Twas grace that taught my heart to fear, and grace my fears relieved." If the Bible speaks truly, God does not bring us to this point of misery because he wants us to be miserable. He brings us to this point because we need to get there in order for God to help us. Paul's question, "Who will deliver me from this body of death?" is a cry for help. It is a cry that God is waiting to answer. Paul writes the answer: "Thanks be to God, who delivers me through Jesus Christ our Lord!" (Romans 7:25).

In all of the religions of the world, there is no answer to the question, "How can we be rescued from the misery caused by selfishness and sin?" that compares to the answer found in Jesus Christ. We see him, the Son of God, hanging on the cross dying for our sins. It is a scene unlike any other in the history of the world. In it, God simultaneously demonstrates on the one hand, his hatred of the sin and selfishness that infects our lives, and on the other hand his love for each one of us.

When we are brought to this place of misery we wonder, "Will God forgive me for what I have done? Can God ever forgive me?" Christianity answers, "Yes." Jesus, the Son of God, died on the cross so that we might be forgiven. He bore the penalty for all our sin. And after he died, he rose from the dead, demonstrating that the penalty had been paid. Through Jesus' death, God's wrath was forever resolved for all who desire God's forgiveness. And for all who desire his forgiveness, there is thereafter only one thing that they receive from God: his love.

Jesus said:

> Blessed are the poor in spirit,
> for theirs is the kingdom of heaven.

> Blessed are those who mourn,
> for they will be comforted.

> Blessed are the meek,
>> for they will inherit the earth.
>
> Blessed are those who hunger and thirst for righteousness,
>> for they will be filled. (Matthew 5:3-6)

Jesus perfectly described our state when we come to the point of misery about which Paul wrote. When we get to that point, we are poor in spirit, because we realize that we have a problem that we cannot solve. We mourn, because we see that we cannot please God. We are meek, knowing that we have no right to make any demands on God—we can only seek his mercy. And we long for the righteousness that we know that God desires, but that we are unable to achieve.

Despite the pitiful condition that we are in, Jesus calls us "blessed." It is here, when we find ourselves in this lowly state, that God bestows his love. It is from here that we enter the kingdom of heaven. Here is where we find comfort from God. From here, we will inherit the new earth that is to come. Here we are declared to be righteous—the righteousness that comes from the work of Jesus, our Lord. Here is the narrow gate.

CHAPTER 3

The Plan of God

Let us consider the possibility that this is true: namely, that God is calling us to repent of our sins and accept Jesus as our Savior. And let us ask if this makes sense. Is the plan described by Christianity one that we would expect from a good and loving God?

Atheists argue that even the idea of a good and loving God does not make sense. They argue that no good God would have created a world in which there is so much pain and suffering. Is there a reasonable response to this assertion? Is it possible, consistent with what Christianity teaches, to come to a reasonable explanation for why a good and loving God would have created this world?

Obviously, we must approach such questions humbly. But in seeking answers, we do not need to presumptuously claim that we can read the mind of God beyond what he has revealed in the Bible, assuming he has spoken in the Bible. To refute the atheist's claim that no God would have created this pain-filled world, we need only to give a reasonable and possible explanation for why a good God would have created this world. If we can do this—give a reasonable and possible explanation—we will have defeated the atheist's argument that no explanation is possible. If Christianity speaks truth, we can expect that God's reasons for doing things the way He is doing them are much better than anything we can possibly understand or articulate. But if we can articulate a reasonable explanation—inadequate as it may be—for why God is doing things in the way Christianity describes, we will have shown that Christianity does make sense.

Why did God Create this Pain-filled World?

So let us ask: "Why was it necessary for God to create the pain-filled world in which we are living?" The book of Christianity, the Bible, teaches that in the end times God is going to bring an end to this world and create a new heavens and a new earth. That new heavens and new earth will be a place without pain, suffering, or death (Revelation 21:1-5). Everyone who is there will live with God forever in a place of perfect peace. So why, we might ask, didn't God just create that place to begin with? If he has all knowledge and all power, as Christianity maintains, why did he not just skip this pain-filled world and give us that paradise?

To begin to answer this question, let us look to the events that transpired in the Garden of Gethsemane on the evening before Jesus was crucified. At that time, Jesus prayed to God the Father asking if there were not some other way. Jesus had previously taught on numerous occasions that he was going to have to die. He even taught that dying was the reason why he came to earth. But when the moment arrived and his death was imminent, he told his disciples, "My soul is overwhelmed with sorrow to the point of death" (Matthew 26:38). And he prayed, "My Father, if it is possible, may this cup be taken from me. Yet not as I will, but as you will" (Matthew 26:39). If it was the Father's will that he die, Jesus would submit to that will and surrender to death on the cross. But he wanted to know if there was not some other way.

God the Father, to whom Jesus was praying, has, according to Christianity, always known all things. This means that before God created anything, he would have known that his act of creation would in time lead to Jesus being in this garden and praying this prayer. He would have known that Jesus, his Son, would be asking the him, the Father, that he not have to die, not if there was some other way. Jesus, who the Bible teaches is the Son of God and shares the Father's divine nature, would also have known this. He was with the Father before anything was created

(John 1:1-3). Before Jesus became a man, he also knew all things. When he came to earth as a baby in Bethlehem, he gave up his knowledge and power to become one of us. In the Garden of Gethsemane Jesus, as a man, did not know for certain whether there might not be another way. But before he became a man and before anything was created, Jesus also would have known that if he and the Father went ahead and created this world, then prior to his death he would be in the Garden pleading that he would not have to die—not if there was any other way.

What does this tells us? It tells us, if the Bible is speaking the truth, that there must have been no other possible way for God to accomplish what he is going to accomplish.. It seems inconceivable that the Father and Son would have gone through with their plan in creating this world if there was any other alternative. It is inconceivable that God did not take into account Jesus' prayer before he created this world.

The profound implication of this seems to be clear. It strongly suggests that even an all-powerful and all-knowing God could not accomplish what God is ultimately going to accomplish, without the events that are taking place in this pain-filled world. This world in which the Son of God had to die, must be a necessary prelude to the new earth that God will create when he brings this world to an end. In other words, there is no other possible world that God could have created which, first, would have accomplished what God has set out to accomplish and, second, would not have required Jesus to die. If there had been such a possible world, God would certainly have created it, instead of this one.

If this is correct, then the hard realities of this pain-filled world do not exist because God does not care. This world does not exist because it just happened. It exists because God has created it and allowed it to exist as part of a plan. If God is good, as Christianity maintains, he does not want anyone to suffer needlessly. There must be a reason for the fact that a good God not only allowed his Son to come and die on the cross, but also allowed us to be born into this pain-filled world, a world in which we and everyone else who has ever lived has endured suffering. Something must be happening here in this world that had to happen before God could finally create the paradise that is to come.

What is it? What is it that is happening here that is so essential?

To try to determine what it could be, let us look more closely at God. Let us see what the Bible says about who God is and what is important to him. Maybe by better understanding God we will be better able to understand what he would be seeking to achieve through the events that are taking place in this world.

God is Love

When we look to the Bible to discover who God is, we find the answer in a simple verse: "God is love" (1 John 4:8). While God knows all things and has the power to do all possible things, the Bible never says, "God is knowledge" or "God is power." In saying, "God is love," the Bible indicates that love defines God more than anything else.

God has always been able to give and receive love because God is actually three persons. When the Bible refers to God it is most often referring to God the Father. God the Father, however, as mentioned above, is not alone—he shares his divine nature with the Son. He also shares it with the Spirit. These three persons—God the Father, God the Son, and God the Spirit—comprise the Trinity. The members of the Trinity have always existed and have always loved each other.

While each of the three persons of the Trinity has all knowledge and all power, one of the members of the Trinity gave up his knowledge and his power for a time, and still remained God. The Son gave up those attributes when he was born as a human baby. Jesus started his life like each of us has started our lives—with no knowledge and with no power. He did not need his power or his knowledge to be God. As Jesus grew, central to his life was not his power or his knowledge; rather, central to his life was love.

Jesus taught that there are two great commandments that form the basis for all that God asks of us. The first is that we are to love the Lord our God with all our heart, with all our soul and with all our mind. The second is that we are to love our neighbor as ourself (Mark 12:28-31). Jesus, according to the Bible, obeyed these commands perfectly. He never failed to perfectly love God or the people around him. Failure to do either is sin; Jesus never sinned.

Through Jesus' life, we learn of the love that he shared with the Father. That love was such that Jesus could say, "I am in the Father and . . . the Father is in me" (John 14:11). During Jesus' final night with his disciples before he died, he told them:

> As the Father has loved me, so I have loved you. Now remain in my love. If you keep my commands, you will remain in my love, just as I have kept my Father's commands and remain in his love. I have told you this so that my joy may be in you and that your joy may be complete. My command is this: Love each other as I have loved you. Greater love has no one than this: to lay down one's life for one's friends. You are my friends if you do what I command . . . This is my command: Love each other. (John 15:9-14, 17)

The love that the Father had shown Jesus was the love that Jesus in turn showed the disciples. And just as Jesus' love for the Father had led him to obey the Father, Jesus asked his disciples to show their love for him by obeying his commands. And what was his command? It was that they love each other. As such, the joy that Jesus knew as a result of the love that he shared with the Father was a joy that he longed for his disciples to also know through their acts of love shown toward one another.

Later that night Jesus prayed to the Father as follows:

> My prayer is not for them alone. I pray also for those who will believe in me through their message, that all of them may be one, Father, just as you are in me and I am in you. May they also be in us so that the world may believe that you have sent me. I have given them the glory that you gave me, that they may be one as we are one—I in them and you in me—so that they may be brought to complete unity. Then the world will know that you sent me and have loved them even as you have loved me. (John 17:20-23)

Jesus is praying here for all those who would become Christians, and his prayer is that they might know the unity that comes from love. He wants them to know that unity in the same way that he knows complete unity with the Father.

The Scriptures speak of the Lord being one. Here the Son explains how the three persons who comprise God are one: The love they have for each other gives them a perfect unity in all things.

A Goal Based in Love

Clearly, then, the most important attribute of God is love. It follows from this that the most important aspect of life in the new earth that God is going to create will be love: everyone will always love God and always love each other. There will be no sin, selfishness or even any temptation to sin or selfishness there. It is also true that there will be no pain, suffering, sickness or death, and that will truly be wonderful. But more wonderful still is that everyone there will be forever living lives of love in perfect unity.

How will God accomplish this? When Christians are brought to the new earth, what will keep them from sinning? Will God rewire them in such a way that it will be impossible for them to sin? Will their new minds and bodies be restructured such that they will only be able to choose love, and not be able to choose selfishness? While it would be a mistake to be too dogmatic, there is reason to question whether this would be possible even for God.[1]

---

[1] Even God cannot do logically inconsistent things, such as making square circles. Maybe in a similar way the nature of love is such that it always involves a free choice.

If the Bible speaks truly about Adam and Eve, they were created in his image (Genesis 1:27). Being made in his image, they had the ability to love God. But they also had another ability—an ability which they exercised—to choose *not* to love God. Could God have created Adam and Eve and everyone else with only the ability to love and not the ability not to love? If Adam and Eve had been created with only the ability to love God, they could never have fallen into sin. If God could have done this—and saved the world from falling into sin, and saved Jesus from his death on the cross—we might wonder why he did not. Perhaps he did not do this because it is impossible even for God. Perhaps love is always a choice. Perhaps in order to love, one must need to reject its opposite, selfishness.

As mentioned at the outset, we do not need to ultimately determine these matters. We are looking only for a possible and reasonable explanation for why God is doing things the way he is. And such an explanation does arise from the idea that in the paradise that is to come, human beings by their very nature may still have the capacity for sin and selfishness. If the Bible speaks truly we know that all who are there—even if they have the capacity for selfishness and sin—will never be tempted by either ever again. Perhaps the events that are taking place in this world are necessary to forever remove that temptation.

A Plan Based in Love

In considering how this might be so, let us begin by going back to the time before God created anything and consider what the members of the Trinity may have been thinking. For them, the love that they had always shared would obviously have been the most important part of each of their existences. It would always have been the source of their greatest joy. Central to their plan in creating this world would have been their knowledge that they could create finite beings in their image who would also have the capacity for love. Having the capacity for love, these beings would have the capacity to know the joy that comes from love; the same joy that the members of the Trinity knew.

But they obviously knew there would be a problem. Being finite, these beings would not have the divine capacity to know all things. And without this divine perspective, even what they did know, they could come to doubt. And there was one important thing that they could not know in the same way that the members of the Trinity have always known it: each member of the Trinity has always known that nothing good is ever gained by selfishness. Knowing all things, they each have always known this with certainty—it is something that they would have never doubted. As such, they have never been tempted to act selfishly towards one another.[2] God the Father, God the Son, and God the Holy Spirit have always known that if any of them acted selfishly towards the others, it would destroy everything. It would be the death of the perfect unity that they have always known. For them, selfishness has never contained any allure. It has been the most hateful thing imaginable.

They would also have known that for finite creatures these things would not be evident in the same way. Finite creatures could be told about selfishness and how it destroys everything. They could come to believe it, but they would not know it with the same certainty that the members of the Trinity have always known it. They might, at times, have doubts about whether there is really nothing to be gained by acting selfishly. In the midst of their doubts, they might make a choice to act selfishly. In putting themselves before God or before one another, they would destroy what their lives and relationships could be. And by engaging in selfishness they would render it impossible to continue to share in the fellowship of the Trinity. Just as the members of the Trinity would never consider tolerating selfishness amongst themselves, so also they would have no interest in maintaining fellowship with finite beings who tolerated and

---

[2] The only exception to this would be when Jesus became one of us. At that point he gave up his omniscience, and was tempted in every way like we are tempted. Unlike us, however, he never sinned.

engaged in it. For the members of the Trinity, what possible joy or value would there be in relationships not centered in love? For the three, whose joy has always depended completely on love, it would be unthinkable to accept into their midst beings who considered it more important to please themselves than to please God or to please each other.

This then is the challenge the Trinity faced. They could create beings who could know the joy of love, but who, being finite, would be tempted not to love. Could anything be done about this? Was there any way to bring these beings to a point to where they, like the members of the Trinity, would never be tempted to put themselves before God or each other? Forcing or manipulating these creatures into loving God and each other before themselves would not work. The love that the members of the Trinity have always known is a love that is freely given. It is not forced or in any way manipulated. The only way these finite beings would be able to enjoy love in the same way that the members of the Trinity know it would be if they could be brought to a point from which they too would know with certainty that nothing good can ever be gained from selfishness. If they could be brought to the point where they were convinced that nothing good could ever come from selfishness, they too could never be tempted. And never being tempted, they would know the joy of love in the same way that the members of the Trinity know it. And it would be possible for them to forever enjoy the fellowship of the Father, Son, and Spirit.

A Plan Implemented

Is there any way that human beings could be brought to such a place? If Christianity speaks truth, then we see the Trinity's solution to this problem being worked out in the world we live in. It is a solution that is painful for God himself as well as humans. But it is a solution that will allow every man and woman who loves God to live with the members of the Trinity forever. The solution to the problem started when God let human beings become selfish. He *made* us to love, but he *let* us become selfish.

If the Bible's story of Adam and Eve is historically true, it began in the Garden of Eden. God put Adam and Eve into a paradise that they could enjoy. He asked only one thing of them: that they not eat of the tree of the knowledge of good and evil. He told them that if they ate of it they would die. The serpent tempted them to eat of it, saying, "You will not certainly die . . . for God knows that when you eat from it your eyes will be opened, and you will be like God, knowing good and evil" (Genesis 3:4-5). They ate from the tree, and they disobeyed God. The serpent's lie had been that they would not die. After they had eaten from the tree, God agreed with the other part of the serpent's statement. God said, "The man has now become like one of us, knowing good and evil" (Genesis 3:22). God knew about the destructive power of evil because he knows all things. We know about the destructive power of evil because we have experienced it. And since that time, this knowledge of good and evil has come to every member of the human race.

Consider this analogy: it as if God let all of us get muddy, and two important things come about as a result. First, each of us has to decide how we feel about the mud. Some of us do not mind the mud; in fact, we rather enjoy playing in it. But others of us do not like mud. We would like to be clean. We discover, however, that we cannot get this mud off. If we call out to God, however, asking him to clean us, he will do it. He knows how to clean us. For those of us who want to be clean, another important thing happens once we are clean: we remember what it was like to be muddy. Our memory of the mud, and the love that God showed towards us in bringing us out of the mud, will keep us from ever wanting to get muddy again.

Consider a king who has allowed a rebellion to take place, and since it began everyone has rebelled. The king has the power to immediately stop the rebellion, but he has let it go on for many years. He has let this happen because although he is a king, he is not a tyrant. He loves his subjects and he wants them to love him. He knows that many of his people will come to regret their rebellion and will turn from their wicked ways and return to him. His plan is to forever reign as a beneficent king over all those who want him to be their king. When he re-establishes his kingdom it will include everyone who—in despair over their the raging rebellion—comes to repent of their own participation in it. The king knows that their memory of the horrors of the rebellion will keep them from wanting to ever rebel again.

However, the king cannot simply ignore the rebellion or act as if the rebellion never happened. In the kingdom that is to come, he knows that it will be necessary for his subjects to respect and obey him. In rebelling against him, his subjects have failed to do the very thing that will make the new kingdom thrive for everyone, king and subjects alike. Accordingly, he has always fiercely hated the rebellion. The anarchy that arose in the rebellion has led to untold suffering and resulted in unspeakable cruelty. The king, in loving his subjects, in his desire to forgive them, could not do so in a way that would leave his hatred of their rebellion ambiguous.

At this point the story diverges from being parallel to a human king in an earthly kingdom, because what God did to solve this problem is something that no human king would or could ever do. God, the Trinity, masterminded a cosmically unselfish act: Jesus the Son would sacrifice himself, dying in our place, to bear God's wrath at our rebellion. Being not only man, but also infinite God, Jesus could die on behalf of everyone who would call him Savior. Despite the Father's love for the Son, he could accept the Son's sacrifice because of two things: first, the Father loved the people he had created and knew that this sacrifice would be the basis of their salvation. Second, he knew that the Son would not stay dead. He knew he would raise the Son to life. He knew that in the new heavens and the new earth, Jesus would forever be praised by everyone who accepted his free gift of salvation.

When God allowed his Son to die for us, God demonstrated how much he hates the sin and selfishness of our lives. For God our sin is no small matter; it is an issue so huge that only the death of the Son of God on the cross could solve it. But by sending his Son to die for us, the Father also showed how much he loves us. God the Father loved us enough to let his son suffer on our behalf. And God the Son loved us enough to endure in our place the pain of a horrible death. But the Son is no longer dead. He is alive, offering us a new life by what he has done.

God did all this knowing that these things were necessary. If he was going to bring finite creatures made in his image to a point that they could live with him forever, there was no other way. He knew that under this plan he could make us fit to live with him in the new earth. All we would have to do is repent and accept the work of the Savior that he provided for us. By repenting, we would in essence be inviting God to change us. And God knew that if we wanted him to change us, he could, and would, do it.

When God brings this world to an end, and creates the new heavens and the new earth, he will give us new bodies. These bodies will be completely free from the slavery to sin that we know in this world. We will be given a fresh start. Although there will be no one to tempt us in the new earth, even if there was, we would no longer be foolishly naïve, like Adam and Eve were. They had no idea what they were getting into, and were easily deceived. We, however, know from firsthand experience where the serpent's path leads. We see it around us every day of our lives.

Although we will be entirely free, as free as we are in this world, the idea of putting ourselves before God or before each other will never enter our minds. We will be living in the visible, tangible presence of the Father and of the Son, knowing what it is to directly feel their love. We will be sharing in the love of all who are there. The idea of ever again choosing to engage in behavior that caused so much pain not only to ourselves but to our Savior will be unthinkable. Our memory of muddiness of this world, and of the efforts that God made to cleanse us from the mud, will keep us from ever wanting to get muddy again.

The Bible says that God works all things for good for those who love him (Romans 8:28). Amongst the "all things" that will be for our good is the pain of this world. In the paradise to come, we will be completely healed from our sufferings here. Our memory of that suffering will completely free us in the lives we lead in the new world from any temptation to depart from the lives of love we will know there. This is a plan worthy of a good and loving God.

CHAPTER 4

The Judgment of God

We have been considering the possibility that Christianity is true, and we have been asking if it makes sense. In asking this, we are essentially trying to understand whether a good God would have done things in the way that Christianity describes. As part of this consideration we need to address the hardest part of the Christian message: the judgment of God.

Christianity has traditionally maintained that when God brings this world to an end he will judge the world. All those who have repented and who have accepted Jesus as their Savior will be forgiven. God will transform them into beings that will be brought to a new earth, where they will spend eternity enjoying life in the presence of God. All those who have not repented, Christianity has traditionally maintained, God will condemn. Jesus himself said, "unless you repent, you too will all perish" (Luke 13:3).

This latter belief strikes many, if not most, of us as unacceptable. It is a belief that seems to epitomize all that is bad about religion.

We hate it when people, in the name of religion, tell outsiders that "if you refuse to believe what we believe, you will be condemned." We want to dismiss such views as something that a good God, especially a God of love, would not be a part of. The Christian assertion that "you need to repent and believe in Jesus or you will be condemned" appears to embody this kind of intolerance.

Most of us, nevertheless, can accept the idea that God should condemn at least some people. Adolph Hitler, most of us would agree, deserves the hottest fires of hell. So do suicide bombers, child molesters, and mass murderers. If God is good, then he cannot ignore what truly evil people do. Our sense of what is right includes a sense that for such people, justice must be done.

But while we can accept God's condemnation of people like that, it is altogether different to assert, as Christianity has traditionally asserted, that God will condemn all those who have not repented. We all know many people—perhaps including ourselves—who have not repented. By and large, this does not seem to be such a bad group of people. Most of them live lives that are similar to the lives of those who have repented. Often they live *better* lives. As we look at them, we do not generally see anything worthy of God's condemnation. Sure, they are not perfect. None of us are. They have often been selfish and we have been angry at some of them for their selfishness. But we can get over it. Are we supposed to believe that God can't? Most of the time most of them, though unrepentant, seem to be trying to do the right thing. We would not condemn them. Would God?

From our perspective, the Bible has God condemning the wrong people. He is putting the dividing line in the wrong place. He should condemn those who are truly evil. He should not condemn people who, from all appearances, live basically good lives. If, as the Bible asserts, he will condemn all those who have not repented and not accepted Jesus as their Savior, he will be condemning a lot of people who look to be living basically decent lives. How could a good God do that?

We Are Not to Comdemn.

As we consider this, we should begin by noting that our reaction—that we would not want God to condemn most people—is just what the Bible says it should be. We are not to judge others. Jesus said:

> Do not judge, or you too will be judged. For in the same way you judge others, you will be

> judged, and with the measure you use, it will be measured to you.
>
> Why do you look at the speck of sawdust in your brother's eye and pay no attention to the plank in your own eye? How can you say to your brother, "Let me take the speck out of your eye," when all the time there is a plank in your own eye? You hypocrite, first take the plank out of your own eye, and then you will see clearly to remove the speck from your brother's eye. (Matthew 7:1-5)

Jesus tells us why we should not judge others. We are not competent to do so—we have a plank in our eye. But he says that God will judge. God does not have a plank in his eye. As we will consider further shortly, the Bible asserts that he will judge each of us by the judgments we have made of others.

But as for us, not only is it not up to us to judge anyone, we are also not to hate anyone. Jesus taught:

> You have heard that it was said, "Love your neighbor and hate your enemy." But I tell you, love your enemies and pray for those who persecute you, that you may be children of your Father in heaven. He causes his sun to rise on

the evil and the good, and sends rain on the righteous and the unrighteous. If you love those who love you, what reward will you get? Are not even the tax collectors doing that? And if you greet only your people, what are you doing more than others? Do not even pagans do that? Be perfect, therefore, as your heavenly Father is perfect. (Matthew 5:43-48)

Since God is being benevolent to both the evil and the good—providing the sun and the rain for both—how can we wish evil on anyone? We should never wish for the condemnation of anyone. We should love and pray for even our enemies. We are to leave matters of justice in God's hands. As the Apostle Paul said,

> Do not take revenge, my friends, but leave room for God's wrath, for it is written: It is mine to avenge; I will repay," says the Lord. On the contrary:
> If your enemy is hungry, feed him;
> > if he is thirsty, give him something
> > to drink.
> In doing this, you will heap burning coals on
> his head.
> Do not be overcome by evil, but overcome evil by good. (Romans 12:19-21)

In the midst of our anger at others over what they've done to us or to others, we are not to condemn or hate. We are to trust God and we are to continue being good to everyone.

So when we conclude that we would not condemn the people we see around us, our attitude is what it should be. We should not want anyone to be condemned. In fact, if the prophet Ezekiel is correct, neither does God. The prophet, speaking for God, said:, "I take no pleasure in the death of the wicked, but rather that they turn from their ways and live" (Ezekiel 33:11). If God takes no pleasure in the death of the wicked, he must take no pleasure in their condemnation.

But, as mentioned, Jesus taught "unless you repent, you too will all perish" (Luke 13:3). He also taught that God was a God of love. Are these things inconsistent? If they both are true, then we would expect that God's condemnation will be three things: (1) fair, (2) not inconsistent with love, and (3) necessary. Our task then is to consider whether, despite our disinclination to believe it, God's judgment of the unrepentant could be all of those things: necessary, fair, and consistent with God being a God of love.

God Hates Selfishness

It is not inconsistent with the idea that God is love for God to hate selfishness. As we considered previously, the joy that each of the members of the Trinity knows arises from the love that they share with each other. For them, selfishness is the most detestable thing imaginable. Selfishness would destroy the perfect unity that they have always known with each other. The members of the Trinity hate selfishness because they love the love they share with each other.

When the members of the Trinity made us in their image, they made us so that we would, like them, live lives of love. To be part of their fellowship, this is how we would need to live. If Christianity speaks truth, then in the new earth, we will be able to live this way. But in this world, this is not how we have lived. We have lived selfishly—putting ourselves before God and before each other. In living this way, we are not fit to live with God:

> You are not a God who is pleased with wickedness;
> > with you, evil people are not welcome.
> The arrogant cannot stand in your presence.
> > You hate all who do wrong. (Psalm 5:4-5)

God hates the selfishness of our lives. It is absolutely antithetical to who he is and what he's about. He is not going to let us live in his presence behaving as we do.

The Apostle Paul said that we are under the wrath of God. He wrote as follows:

> The wrath of God is being revealed from heaven against all the godlessness and wickedness of people, who suppress the truth by their wickedness, since what may be known about God is plain to them, because God has made it plain to them. For since the creation of the world God's invisible qualities—his eternal power and divine nature—have been clearly seen, being understood from what has been made, so that people are without excuse. (Romans 1:18-20)

If what Paul is saying is true, it is not a coincidence that most people believe that God exists. God has made it clear that he exists. Paul says that not only do we know he exists, we know something of what he is like.

We Know God Exists

God's existence, according to Paul, is apparent from the things that God has made. The most amazing thing God has made is us. The Bible asserts that God made us in his likeness. We can see, if the Bible is true, that he made us very much like the members of the Trinity. He made us so much like the members of the Trinity that one of them, the Son, could become one of us and yet still be God. He also made us so much like the members of the Trinity that we might enjoy in our lives that which they enjoy most in theirs—the joy that comes from love. One of the things that tells us that God exists is the joy we experience when we give and receive love.

Some people use the theory of evolution to argue that there is no God.[3] They assert that everything that has happened here is the result of blind, random chance in a godless universe. They look at who we are as human beings and conclude that we are not as special as we think. It is remarkable, they say, what evolution has done, but we are nevertheless an accident. When they look at the joy that we can know in our lives from love, they say the same thing: it is just an accident of evolution

In contrast, if the Bible is true, the joy that we can know from love is the exact opposite of an accident: it is God's gift to us of the most special thing in God's existence. The gift that the members of the Trinity endow to us is wonderful beyond words as it reflects the best part of their communal experience. When we call love an accident—that which is the most special thing in both our existence and God's existence— we are being profoundly ungrateful. We are also lying to ourselves.

---

3   Obviously, believing in evolution does not make one an atheist. Some believe, and others allow the possibility, that God is working through evolutionary processes. See, e.g., Plantinga, *Where the Conflict Really Lies* (Oxford University Press, 2011)

If the Apostle Paul is correct, at some level we know that what we experience in this world is no accident. On some level we know that there has to be a God who is responsible for, among other things, the way we feel when we experience the love and kindness of others. We can tell ourselves that these feelings are an accident that somehow just happened in a godless universe. But on some level, if Paul is correct, we know better.

Paul wrote:

> For although they knew God, they neither glorified him as God nor gave thanks to him, but their thinking became futile and their foolish hearts were darkened. Although they claimed to be wise, they became fools and exchanged the glory of the immortal God for images made to look like a mortal human being and birds and animals and reptiles. (Romans 1:21-23)

According to Paul, we all innately know enough about God to know that we should be thanking and praising him for creating us to be the way we are and to live in the world that we live in. However, instead of thanking and praising God, he says we have created other gods to worship. An example of a person doing this is found in Isaiah 44:14-20:

The Judgment of God

He cut down cedars,
> or perhaps took a cypress or oak. . . .

It is used as fuel for burning;
> some of it he takes and warms himself,
> he kindles a fire and bakes bread.

But he also fashions a god and worships it;
> he makes an idol and bows down to it.

Half of the wood he burns in the fire;
> over it he prepares his meal,
> he roasts his meat and eats his fill.

He also warms himself and says,
> "Ah! I am warm; I see the fire."

From the rest he makes his god, his idol;
> he bows down to it and worships.

He prays to it and says,
> "Save me! You are my god!"

They know nothing, they understand nothing;
> their eyes are plastered over so they cannot see,
> and their minds closed so they cannot understand.

No one stops to think,
> no one has the knowledge or understanding to say,

"Half of it I used for fuel;
> I even baked bread over its coals,
> I roasted meat and I ate.

Shall I make a detestable thing from what is left?
> Shall I bow down to a block of wood?"

Such a person feeds on ashes, a deluded heart misleads him;
> he cannot save himself, or say,
> "Is not this thing in my right hand a lie?"

What a pitiful scene. What obvious foolishness: he uses half of the block of wood for cooking and the other half to make a god. Can't he see he is holding a lie?

But don't we do the same thing? We do not, of course, worship blocks of wood, but we encourage people to believe whatever they want about God. It does not matter if it is true. All that matters is that they find a god or a religion that pleases them. We are too sophisticated to worship blocks of wood, but aren't we just as foolish as the person who does?

We Know How God Wants Us to Live

Paul asserts that not only do we know that God exists, but we also know his moral law, which has been written on our hearts. God gave us a conscience (Romans 2:14-15). We, however, use it in a way that God did not intend. We use our conscience to identify the good things we have done, compare them to the bad, and conclude that we are, on balance, pretty good. Paul says that our conscience should lead us in a different direction. In a passage that is true of both the law of God written in our conscience and the law of God as contained in the Bible, Paul writes:

> Now we know that whatever the law says, it says . . . so that every mouth may be silenced and the whole world held accountable to God. Therefore no one will be declared righteous in his sight by the works of the law; rather, through the law we become conscious of our sin. (Romans 3:19-20)

If we were to use our conscience—the law of God written on our hearts—correctly, we would see that it does not exist to indicate how "good" we have been. It instead tells us that our lives are full of selfishness. It tells us we are sinners who are guilty before God.

When God judges us, he will not, according to the Bible, judge us based on some law that we do not know. God will not pull out the Bible and read its commands to us if we know nothing of the Bible. Instead, we will all be judged by what we do know. Our consciences have taught us about right and wrong. We have each demonstrated that we have learned from our consciences by the moral judgments we have made of other people. Those judgments will be the basis by which we will be judged. Jesus, as previously quoted, said, "in the same way you judge others, you will be judged" (Matthew 7:2). To the same effect, God said, through one of the prophets, "by their own standards I will judge them" (Ezekiel 7:27). The Apostle Paul made clear how this will work when he wrote:

> You, therefore, have no excuse, you who pass judgment on someone else, for at whatever point you judge the other, you are condemning yourself, because you who pass judgment do the same things. Now we know that God's judgment against those who do such things is based on truth. So when you, a mere human being, pass judgment on them and yet do the same things, do you think you will escape God's judgment? Or do you show contempt for the riches of his kindness, forbearance and patience, not realizing that God's kindness is intended to lead you to repentance? (Romans 2:1-4)

Paul says that when we judge another, we condemn ourselves, because we do the same things we condemn in the person we judge. At the last judgment we might imagine God in essence playing a video of the judgments that each of us has made of other people. And then he will ask us, "Have you done what you condemned in that person? Or in that other person? Or in that one?" The answer will be obvious. We will all be speechless. None of us has lived up to the moral standards by which we have judged other people. And then we can imagine God asking those who have not repented, "Did you not know that I patiently waited for you to repent? I gave you all those years, full of many good things, in which I wanted you to come to me. And I gave you my Son who died on your behalf. It was obvious what you needed to do. Why did you not do it?" And what then can we say? There will be no answer. There is no possible answer.

This chapter started by noting how we hate the intolerance of people who in the name of religion tell others that God will condemn them. If Paul, however, is right, no one needs to tell us anything. The facts are in front of our faces. Our conscience says it. The judgments we have made of others confirms it. If we would open our eyes we would see that God has reason to be angry with us. There is nothing unfair about his judgment.

The message of Christianity is that there is nevertheless hope for us. Jesus said he did not come to earth to condemn the world but to save the world:

> For God did not send his Son into the world to condemn the world, but to save the world through him. Whoever believes in him is not condemned, but whoever does not believe stands condemned already because they have not believed in the name of God's one and only Son. This is the verdict: Light has come into the world, but people loved darkness instead of light because their deeds were evil. Everyone who does evil hates the light, and will not come into the light for fear that their deeds will be exposed. But whoever lives by the truth comes into the light, so that it may be seen plainly that what they have done has been done in the sight of God. (John 3:17-21)

Jesus came as a means of salvation. Those who do not believe in Jesus are condemned not because of what Jesus did. They are condemned because they need a Savior, and in rejecting Jesus, they have rejected the one God has sent to be their Savior. Why would anyone do such a thing? Jesus explains that people will stay in the darkness to hide their evil deeds. For all who come to the light, however, there is eternal life.

We tend to think that we are being very tolerant when we make such statements as "all religions lead to God." If what Paul asserts is true, then the one who is really being tolerant is God. He says, "do you show contempt for the riches of his kindness, forbearance and patience, not realizing that God's kindness is intended to lead you to repentance?" (Romans 2:4). The Apostle Peter said the same thing: "He is patient with you, not wanting anyone to perish, but everyone to come to repentance" (2 Peter 3:9). According to the Bible, it is obvious God exists. It is also obvious that we have done wrong. God is giving us time. He is being patient. He is waiting. Are we going to come to our senses?

Is God Fair?

But some might object that this is not fair. What about all the good things we have done in our lives? Don't those things matter? Why doesn't God just weigh the good that we have done against the bad, and see which way the scale tips?

If the Bible speaks truly, God is not looking for pretty good people who he can take to a pretty good place to live pretty good lives. God is looking for those he can transform into people who will be perfect, so that he can bring them to live with him forever. What prevents us from being suitable to living our life with God is not that the scale of our good deeds versus our bad tips a little this way or that. The thing that prevents us from being suitable is that there is any bad in us at all. God has made a way to solve the problem of all that is wrong in us, but he needs one thing—he needs us to ask him.

God is not looking for good people; there are, by God's standards, no good people. He needs people who can look at themselves as God looks at them and acknowledge their sin and their selfishness. He desires that they repent, and in repenting, to ask him to make them clean. He is not going to force himself on anyone. But for anyone who wants it, he will cleanse them from all that makes them dirty.

For those who do repent, it is not as if their repentance establishes that they are good people who deserve to live in God's presence. Not one human deserves to live in God's presence. Rather, those who repent acknowledge that they deserve God's condemnation. They call out to him for mercy. In doing so, they see that God has provided for their salvation through his Son, who died to bear the condemnation that they deserved. In accepting Jesus as Savior they are putting their faith in God. They are trusting God and in his plan of salvation.

Doesn't the Good We Have Done Matter?

But does not the good we have done in our lives count at all? What about a person who has done lots of good in their life, and not very much bad? Even though they have not repented, isn't such a person in some sense a good person? How can God condemn such a person?

But this is essentially to argue that God should tolerate a little selfishness. In every seemingly good person, there is some selfishness. And that is the issue for a perfect God who cannot abide selfishness.

Let us ask, if a person, even a "good" person, has not repented, why have they not repented? Is there any good excuse a person can give for refusing God's good gift of salvation? If what the Bible says is true, then we all know that God exists. We also all know that we have done wrong. If I did not know God exists, I would have an excuse. If I did not know I had done wrong in my life, I would have another excuse. But if what the Bible says is true, none of us has either of these excuses. Both God's existence, and our guilt for having done things we know to be wrong, are as plain as day. What possible excuse reason do we have for ignoring these realities? What possible excuse can we give for not saying, "God, please forgive me"?

And if we have heard the story of Jesus dying on the cross for the sins of humanity, how can we just ignore it? How can we say: "I do not need that. I'll get by without that. I will just do a few good deeds to make up for these bad things I have done." We want to think that if we have any problem, it is just a little problem. We want to think we can solve our problem by ourselves. But God demonstrated that our problem is no little problem. when his Son needed to die on our behalf.

If I refuse to bow before the God who has created me, and refuse to humbly ask his forgiveness, can I nevertheless argue that I am a good person? If I repent, I am saying the opposite. I am saying "I am not a good person. I deserve your condemnation. Please forgive me." If I do not repent, when I face God I will be left with the argument, "I am not a bad person. I am a good person. Please treat me well, because I have done a lot of good things in my life." Will God be impressed?

God is the one who has given us all the incentives we have for doing the good things we do in our lives. God has put his law on our hearts. Because of this we, as a rule, feel better about ourselves when we do good, and not so good about ourselves when we do bad. Because of this, others, as a rule, praise us when we are generous, and condemn us when we are selfish. So when we do something good for another person, does this establish that we are good? Is it not possible for us to be good most of the time for entirely selfish reasons? Our lives are generally more pleasant when we act unselfishly. This is because of the way God has made us. Who then deserves the credit for the fact that most of the time we treat others well? Should we congratulate ourselves for this? Or should we praise

God for making us in such a way that even the most selfish of people often behave well?

At a basic level, if I do not repent, is it not because I do not want to bow before God and give him his proper place? God has allowed me to live my life however I want. I can treat my existence as if it were all about me. I can establish my own rules for living. By giving me a conscience, God has made it easier for me to live in a way in which I am usually considerate of others. But I have the freedom to choose when and where I will violate my conscience to get something I want. When I am choosing to do the right thing, I can do it for reasons that have nothing to do with God. There are all sorts of reasons I can do the right thing because I love me.

But God did not make us so that our lives would be about loving ourselves. God made us because he wanted to enter a relationship with us, a relationship in which he will love us and we will love him. He does not, however, throw his pearls to the pigs. When we choose to live for ourselves, caring nothing for him, we will not receive his approval. We will receive his condemnation. He will condemn us because we will have chosen the way of selfishness over the way of love. Because God hates selfishness, he will condemn all of us who, for the entirety of our lives, without remorse or repentance, have embraced the selfishness of our lives.

Regarding what God's condemnation will be like, it will certainly be proportional to what one knows. Jesus said:

> "That servant who knows the master's will and does not get ready or does not do what the master wants will be beaten with many blows. But the one who does not know and does things deserving punishment will be beaten with few blows." (Luke 12:47-48)

Judas, having spent three years with Jesus before he betrayed him, knew very well his master's will. Of him, Jesus said: "[W]oe to that man who betrays the Son of Man! It would be better for him if he had not been born" (Matthew 26:24).[4] Accordingly, whatever God's condemnation is like, it will be fair to everyone.

It is then, first, not inconsistent for a God of love to condemn those of us who refuse to repent of the selfishness of our lives. Second, as we have seen, he will judge us in a way that is entirely fair. He will use our judgments of others

---

4 To this writer's knowledge, the Bible does not say of anyone else that it would be better if they had not been born. While it may be reading too much into this, it raises the question whether others who experience God's condemnation and punishment might nevertheless, despite their suffering, not feel as if it would be better that they had not been born.

to show that each of us knows that we have done wrong. Knowing that we have done wrong, there is no excuse for our failure to repent.

But Is God's Judgment Necessary?

One question, however, remains. Is God's judgment necessary? Even if God's judgment is consistent with his being a God of love, and even if he is going to do it in a way that is entirely fair, is it really necessary for God to condemn those who do not repent?

Two points may be made here. First, God is just. Not only is he a God of love; he is also a God of justice. Nowhere are these two aspects of his nature made more perfectly clear than in Jesus' death on the cross. When Jesus died for our sins, God's justice was satisfied and his love for us made clear. But for those who have not repented and have not accepted what Christ has done on behalf of repentant sinners, God's justice has yet to be satisfied. Because God is not only loving but just, the coming judgment is necessary. God's nature simply will not allow him to ignore the horrors that selfishness and sin have brought to this world.

But a second point can also be made. It is easy for us to assume that God could just bring everyone, repentant and unrepentant, to the paradise that will be the new earth, and everything would be fine. But this assumption bears more investigation. Could the new earth be what it will be if God allowed in both the repentant and the unrepentant?

If we are brought to the new earth after repenting in this world, then we will obtain what we have requested. We will have asked to be forgiven and cleansed from our sin, and in the new earth all of our hopes for living eternally with God will be realized. We will be brought to a place where there is no sin, because everyone will always love God and will always love each other. Most importantly, we will find ourselves in the presence of our God. In the old world we would have, by faith, trusted his promise that if we believe in Jesus we would be forgiven. In the presence of the Trinity we will sense their love in a way that is more immediate than anything we ever knew in our previous existence. Being with them, seeing them as they are, we will never again be tempted to sin. We will remember our old existence and all the pain and suffering that was caused by sin. Every day of our lives in the former world we witnessed the pain and destruction caused by selfishness and sin. When we get to the new earth, nothing could entice us to return to that again.

But then let us consider a hypothetical situation. Try to imagine if we had not repented and were brought to this new earth. We would find ourselves in the presence of a God who we never cared much about. We would also find ourselves in the presence of Jesus who died for sins that we never thought were much of a problem. We will be with people who are thrilled and overwhelmed to be with their Savior. They will have all believed in him in their previous existence and, to an extent, would have known him. We, however, would have never known him, especially not as our Savior. We who never repented in our previous existence would not know what to make of any of this. One thing, however, might strike us as especially significant: everyone in the new world is as free as they had been in the old world. That means we will be able to carry on as we want. The fact that all those who have asked to be cleansed from their sins would never consider sinning again does not mean that we can't. This new place would provide another opportunity for us to live for ourselves. Let us carry on as before.

Obviously the latter scenario is something that will never happen. But it at least highlights the problem. It shows that we are not in any position to draw the conclusion that we tend to draw—that God could just bring everyone to the new earth.

God's creation of the new earth will come at the price of the death of his son. We are in no position to say that in accomplishing this difficult thing, God's exclusion of the unrepentant from the new earth is not necessary. Just as we would not want anyone to perish, God does not want anyone to perish. But if he is going to create a place where all who love him can live with him forever, then God's judgment is necessary. It is not only necessary; it is also fair. And it is not only necessary and fair; it is also consistent with his being a God of love.

God does not throw pearls to the pigs. Instead, he has designed a plan where all those who love him, and love what he loves, will be brought to a place where they can enjoy life with him, with the Son and with the Spirit, forever.

CHAPTER 5

The Life God Offers

Suppose a person decides that yes, Christianity does seem to make sense. And suppose this person also realizes that he or she does believe in a good and loving God. In light of the selfishness in their life, they additionally comes to see themselves as a sinner. And then they pray: "God, if it is true that Jesus Christ really died for a sinner like me, then I want to accept him as my Savior." In making this decision, they have become a Christian. But what is next? What kind of life are they entering into? Is it a life that makes sense? What kind of life can one expect to have as a result of committing to and following a good and loving God? Let us consider at least a few aspects of what the Bible says about the Christian life.

Peace With God

If the Bible speaks truth, then central to the Christian life is that the Christian is at peace with God. Jesus said:

> "Peace I leave with you; my peace I give you. I do not give to you as the world gives. Do not let your hearts be troubled and do not be afraid." (John 14:27)

> "I have told you these things, so that in me you may have peace. In this world you will have trouble. But take heart! I have overcome the world." (John 16:33)

A Christian in this world will have troubles. In the midst of those troubles, however, Jesus commands the Christian not to be troubled. And it makes sense that a Christian should not be troubled because, as Jesus says, no matter what happens in life, the Christian is at peace with God. Jesus, who has already overcome the world through his death and resurrection, will be with the Christian through any trouble.

In Paul's epistle to the Romans—after setting forth his case for the Christian faith in the first four chapters—he starts his description of the life of a Christian in chapter five. He immediately speaks of the peace that the Christian has with God:

> Therefore, since we have been justified through faith, we have peace with God through our Lord Jesus Christ, through whom we have

gained access by faith into the grace in which we now stand. And we boast in the hope of the glory of God. Not only so, but we also glory in our sufferings, because we know that suffering produces perseverance; perseverance, character; and character, hope. And hope does not put us to shame, because God's love has been poured out into our hearts by the Holy Spirit, who has been given to us. (Romans 5:1-5)

The Christian, being at peace with God, and knowing that God is working for the Christian's good, can look at even suffering in an entirely new way. The Christian does not need to bemoan his or her suffering. They can rejoice in it, knowing that in the midst of their suffering the Holy Spirit is working for their good, developing their perseverance, their character and their hope. Indeed, the Christian can rejoice in every circumstance in life because "in all things God works for the good of those who love him, who have been called according to his purpose" (Romans 8:28). If the Bible speaks truth about the way God works in the Christian's life, then God has given the Christian every reason to be continually praising and thanking him.

Paul makes the same point in his letter to the Philippians when he writes:

> Rejoice in the Lord always. I will say it again: Rejoice! Let your gentleness be evident to all. The Lord is near. Do not be anxious about anything, but in every situation, by prayer and petition, with thanksgiving, present your requests to God. And the peace of God, which transcends all understanding, will guard your hearts and your minds in Christ Jesus. (Philippians 4:4-7)

Because the Lord is near, Paul tells believers that there is no need to be anxious about anything. Not anything. Rather in everything, as the Christian prays and petitions God in each situation, he or she is to be rejoicing and thanking God regardless of the difficulty of their circumstances. The Christian can and should rejoice—not just once in a while, and not just over a few things here and there—but always and over every situation.

The only way the Christian can live like this, such that in every circumstance he or she can experience the peace that transcends understanding, is by faith. Paul wrote:

> For in the gospel the righteousness of God is revealed—a righteousness that is by faith from first to last, just as it is written: "The righteous will live by faith." (Romans 1:17)

It is by faith that the Christian is saved, as the Christian, believing in God, looks to Jesus as their Savior. And it is by faith that the Christian is to live, believing in every circumstance in life that God is working his good and loving will within the believer's life.

The Christian's Struggle with Sin

One of the troubles a Christian must face is a continual struggle with sin. When a person becomes a Christian, he or she confesses and renounces the sin in their life. Nevertheless they continue to sin. It is as if sin in some way has corrupted humanity, and in this world, in these bodies, despite our best intentions, the Christian cannot get rid of it. As Paul wrote: "[W]e ourselves, who have the firstfruits of the Spirit, groan inwardly as we wait eagerly for our adoption to sonship, the redemption of our bodies" (Romans 8:23). At the end of time, when God creates the new heaven and the new earth, we will be given glorious new bodies that will be free from slavery to sin. But for now, the Christian struggles with sin. Paul describes it as follows:

> For in my inner being I delight in God's law; but I see another law at work in the members of my body, waging war against the law of my mind and making me a prisoner of the law of sin at

work within my members. (Romans 7:22-23, NIV 1984)

The Christian wants to obey God and to stop sinning. But sin is still there, waging war against their mind and body. Despite their best efforts, they continue to sin.

Yet remember, Jesus commands the Christian not to be troubled. It is not as if the Christian is not to be concerned about the sin in his or her life. They must struggle against it. But in the midst of the struggle, the Christian is to see that sin has lost its real power over them. The greatest power of sin is its ability to separate a person from the love of God. For the Christian, this power is gone. As Paul wrote, "Therefore, there is now no condemnation for those who are in Christ Jesus, because through Christ Jesus the law of the Spirit who gives life has set you free from the law of sin and death (Romans 8:1-2).

Apart from Christ, a life infected with sin would earn God's condemnation and death. It would mean separation from God. Because of Christ, however, sin in the life of a Christian means neither of those things. Sin in the Christian's life is something that the Christian is called to hate and to battle, but it will never have the power to separate the Christian from the love of God.

When the Christian sins, he or she should confess their sin. They should then thank God that they are forgiven.

Seeing that they are forgiven, in gratitude they have reason anew to love Christ. And when they love Christ, Christ says he will do something:

> "Anyone who loves me will obey my teaching. My Father will love them, and we will come to them and make our home with them." (John 14:23)

Jesus says that if we love him, we will obey him. Each time we sin and seek his forgiveness, we have new reason to love him. And when we love him, we obey him. When we obey him, we enjoy fellowship with him and with the Father.

Jesus said, "Let anyone who is thirsty come to me and drink. Whoever believes in me, as Scripture has said, rivers of living water will flow from within them" (John 7:37-38). When we sin, we thirst. When we come to Jesus, he not only quenches our thirst, he causes streams of living water to flow from us.

But then, sooner or later, we sin again. We repent of some sin in the morning, and then by that the afternoon we have done it again. Somehow, in this world, in these bodies, we cannot help ourselves. But our response must always be the same. God is calling us to again have faith in what he has done for us. He is not calling us to engage in endless self-condemnation. Rather, He is calling us to confess our sin and then praise and thank God for forgiving us. We do this again and again, and each time we sin we are to love him anew for his grace in forgiving us. And in loving him, he calls us to obey him. The Christian life is something of a cycle where every sin provides us a reason to come to God, asking him for his forgiveness; and then, in receiving it, to love God anew, and in loving him to once again turn away from sin.

In order for the Christian to fully enjoy this, however, the Christian again needs faith. Paul wrote that "The righteous will live by faith" (Romans 1:17). If we stop living by faith, and we start focusing on the fact that we are not worthy of God's love, given our sin, we will stop thanking and praising God and continue to focus on ourselves. If we find some sin in our life to be particularly disturbing, we can fixate on it, thinking we need to overcome it to show that we love God, in order to continue to know fellowship with God. But that reverses the order of what Jesus has established. To repeat what Jesus said,

> "Anyone who loves me will obey my teaching. My Father will love them, and we will come to them and make our home with them." (John 14:23)

Note the order. We are, first, to love God. Second, in loving him, we are to obey his teaching. Third, as we obey his teaching, we will know fellowship with God.

Christ does not say that *if* we obey him, *then* we will love him. He says that *if* we love him, *then* we will obey him. Our focus should not first be on our battle with some particular sin that we want to stop committing. Our focus should be first on loving Christ. In loving him we will be able to deal with sin. In loving him, we will first of all see that any particular sin we struggle with has no power to separate us from the love of Christ. We will secondly see that to the extent that the sin makes us feel as if Christ were distant (though truly he is not), whatever pleasure the sin seems to offer us, that is nothing that can be compared to knowing Christ's love. Nothing that sin offers can ever compare to the experience of having the Father and the Son make their home with us through the Holy Spirit.

A License to Sin?

But as we consider whether the Christian life makes sense, the objection could be raised that this teaching is nothing but a license to sin. If the Christian is forgiven for every sin and has no risk of losing his or her salvation, then is the Christian free to sin as much as they want? Paul addresses this, saying:

> What shall we say, then? Shall we go on sinning so that grace may increase? By no means! We are

those who have died to sin; how can we live in it any longer? Or don't you know that all of us who were baptized into Christ Jesus were baptized into his death? We were therefore buried with him through baptism into death in order that, just as Christ was raised from the dead through the glory of the Father, we too may live a new life. (Romans 6:1-4)

According to Paul, when we accept Christ as our Savior, we have accepted Christ's death as the basis for our forgiveness. In doing so, we have died to sin. And then, just as Christ rose from the dead, so we too, in Christ, enter a new life. As such, Paul says, "count yourselves dead to sin but alive to God in Christ Jesus" (Romans 6:11). In essence, Paul is telling us that when we accepted Christ as our Savior, we made our decision about sin: we died to it. He then tells us to live like we have died to it.

Paul, after considering the preposterous question, "Shall we go on sinning so that grace may increase?" then asks a subtler one:

> What then? Shall we sin because we are not under law but under grace? (Romans 6:15)

Here the question is not whether we should sin so grace may increase. Rather here he asks whether we should sin because we can; that is, because we will not lose our salvation because of it. He answers:

> By no means! Don't you know that when you offer yourselves to someone as obedient slaves, you are slaves of the one you obey—whether you are slaves to sin, which leads to death, or to obedience, which leads to righteousness? ...
>
> ... When you were slaves to sin, you were free from the control of righteousness. What benefit did you reap at that time from the things you are now ashamed of? Those things result in death! But now that you have been set free from sin and have become slaves of God, the benefit you reap leads to holiness, and the result is eternal life. For the wages of sin is death, but the gift of God is eternal life in Christ Jesus our Lord. (Romans 6:15-16, 20-23)

When we continue to sin, we are bringing death into our lives. Why would we continue to do that? We have been given life. Why would we again choose death? Having known life, through living at peace with God, we know better than to once again choose death.

Chastisement

God does not, and indeed cannot, punish a Christian for sin in his or her life. He cannot because Christ has already paid the price for their sin. As Francis Schaeffer has noted, this is where the justice of God works in our favor.[5] God, being just, cannot punish the same sin twice. God has accepted Christ's sacrifice on the cross as the punishment for the sin of all who look to Christ as Savior. For Christians, God will not punish that sin again.

But this does not mean that God does not care about sin in the Christian's life; it does not mean that he does nothing about it. God chastises those who are his children, just as a loving parent disciplines his or her children:

> My son, do not despise the LORD's discipline
> and do not resent his rebuke,
> because the LORD disciplines those he loves,
> as a father the son he delights in. (Proverbs 3:11-12)

The author of Hebrews writes:

> Endure hardship as discipline; God is treating you as his children. For what children are not disciplined

---

5 Francis A. Schaeffer, *The Finished Work of Christ*, (Wheaton: Crossway Books, 1998), p. 229.

by their father? If you are not disciplined—and everyone undergoes discipline—then you are not legitimate, not true sons and daughters at all. Moreover, we have all had human fathers who disciplined us and we respected them for it. How much more should we submit to the Father of spirits and live! They disciplined us for a little while as they thought best; but God disciplines us for our good, in order that we may share in his holiness. No discipline seems pleasant at the time, but painful. Later on, however, it produces a harvest of righteousness and peace for those who have been trained by it. (Hebrews 12:7-11)

Since God's chastisement is painful, one might ask, is there any real difference between punishment and chastisement? The answer is yes, there is every difference. First, whatever the pain of chastisement may be, it is nothing compared to the punishment that our sins deserve. Second, God chastises a Christian not to punish them, but to help them grow. As the Christian struggles against sin, it is possible for them to see that the pain of chastisement is helpful. As we have noted, a Christian, although having repented of sin, continues to sin, despite their desire that it be out of their life. On the surface, sin is appealing and tempting. But on a deeper level, on the level of their true self, they hate it. Accordingly, it is possible for them, in the midst of the pain of chastisement, to thank God for it. Their pain is helping them to become more the person that, in their innermost being, they truly want to be.

In the quote above the writer of Hebrews says, "Endure hardship as discipline. . ." It is interesting that he does not say that every hardship is actually discipline, but instead that we are to endure it *as if it were* discipline. Paul says, "we also glory in our sufferings" because we know that God is working good in our lives through it (Romans 5:3-5). Whether the hardships in our lives are actually discipline does not really matter. What does matter, however, is that God is working his good in us through whatever hardships we face. If we believe what the Bible is saying, we can rejoice in our hardships, knowing that through them he is helping us to grow into the kind of persons that we really want to be—the kind of persons that God wants us to be.

The Secret of Jesus' Life

Let us now consider how, on a practical level, a Christian is to go about living his or her life day to day? What will enable them to live their life as a follower of God? In answering this, let us first consider how Jesus lived. What was the focus of his life?

The Life God Offers

As we have discussed, Jesus entered this world just as we did. As a baby born in Bethlehem, he did not bring with him the omniscience and omnipotence he had known with the Father before entering Mary's womb. Although he remained a member of the Trinity, he gave up his knowledge and power to become truly human. He was a born a baby just like we once were. He came to earth as a man with no innate supernatural advantages over what any of us have had. So how did he become the person he became? What allowed him to live as he did?

Jesus gives us a clear answer: his life was based on his relationship with the Father. Jesus said:

> Don't you believe that I am in the Father, and that the Father is in me? The words I say to you I do not speak on my own authority. Rather, it is the Father, living in me, who is doing his work. Believe me when I say that I am in the Father and the Father is in me ... (John 14:10-11)

The Father was source of Jesus' teaching:

> For I did not speak on my own, but the Father who sent me commanded me to say all that I have spoken. I know that his command leads to eternal life. So whatever I say is just what the Father has told me to say. (John 12:49-50)

He made clear that nothing he did in his life was done apart from the Father:

> "Very truly I tell you, the Son can do nothing by himself; he can only do what he sees the Father doing, because whatever the Father does the Son also does. For the Father loves the Son and shows him all he does. . . . (John 5:19-20)

Jesus' life was so closely identified with the Father that he could say: "If you knew me, you would know my Father also" (John 8:19).

The miracles were evidence of the Father's work in him:

> [E]ven though you do not believe me, believe the works, that you may know and understand that the Father is in me, and I in the Father. (John 10:38)

When Jesus was arrested in the Garden of Gethsemane one of his disciples cut off the ear of the servant of the high priest. Jesus responded:

> Put your sword back in its place ... for all who draw the sword will die by the sword. Do you think I cannot call on my Father, and he will at once put at my disposal more than twelve legions of angels? (Matthew 26:52-53)

In saying this, Jesus—consistent with his statement that he could do nothing apart from the Father—made plain that it was through the Father that he performed his miracles. Jesus could not have been any clearer: what enabled him to lead the life he led was his relationship with the Father.

Living Through Christ

Now what makes this especially striking and indeed wonderful is that Jesus offers to us this same kind of relationship. Just as the Father lived in him and he in the Father, so it is with us:

> Because I live, you also will live. On that day you will realize that I am in my Father, and you are in me, and I am in you. (John 14:19-20)

And just as Jesus could do nothing apart from the Father, so also Jesus made clear that the Christian can do nothing apart from Jesus:

> I am the vine; you are the branches. If you remain in me and I in you, you will bear much fruit; apart from me you can do nothing. (John 15:5)

And just as the Father showed himself, and what he was doing, to Jesus, so Jesus, through the Holy Spirit, will show himself to us:

> I will ask the Father, and he will give you another advocate to help you and be with you forever—the Spirit of truth. The world cannot accept him, because it neither sees him nor knows him. But you know him, for he lives with you and will be in you. I will not leave you as orphans; I will come to you. Before long, the world will not see me anymore, but you will see me. (John 14:16-19)

Just as the Father taught Jesus the words to say, so Jesus, through the Spirit, told his disciples:

> But the Advocate, the Holy Spirit, whom the Father will send in my name, will teach you all things and will remind you of everything I have said to you. (John 14:26)

Jesus, through the work of the Holy Spirit, promised his disciples that he would teach them "all things."

Jesus makes clear that if we have faith in him, our lives will be like what his life was. He stated:

> Very truly I tell you, whoever believes in me will do the works I have been doing, and they will do even greater things than these, because I am going to the Father. And I will do whatever you ask in my name, so that the Father may be

glorified in the Son. You may ask me for anything in my name, and I will do it. (John 14:12-14)

What an astounding promise: that Jesus will do anything we ask in his name. In making this promise, we can imagine that he was offering us the same thing that he was receiving from the Father. Did not the Father give Jesus all that Jesus asked of him? One might wonder if there was any occasion other than in the Garden of Gethsemane when Jesus asked the Father for something, and the Father did not do it. But even in the Garden, Jesus prayed, "yet not my will, but yours be done" (Luke 22:42). His request that the cup be taken from him was subject to the greater prayer: "your will be done." When Jesus tells us to pray in his name, that too would include our praying, "yet not my will, but your will be done." This does not, however, diminish the fact that whenever we ask Jesus for something that corresponds with Jesus' will, he promises that he will do it.

But how can Jesus say we will do things that are greater than what he did? As we seek to understand this, we should start by recognizing that the miracles that Jesus performed were signs that he was the Messiah. His miraculous healings and bringing people back from the dead had a purpose beyond showing love to those individuals whom he healed. They also showed that he was the Son of God. No one else is the Son of God. There is, therefore, no one else for whom this secondary purpose would come into play. As such, Jesus may do miracles through us in a way different than the way the Father performed miracles through him. Jesus would have no interest in performing miracles through us in a way that would suggest that any of us were the Son of God, because none of us are.

It would make sense, then, that Jesus may often do miracles through us in a way that does not highlight our role in the miracle. And it is not hard to see how this would be for our good. Jesus knew no sin, and accordingly the miracles he performed posed no threat of causing him to develop a self-centered pride. For us, though, if we were to perform miracles in the same way he did, the threat of sinful pride would be real indeed.

Nevertheless, he promises he will grant what we ask, when we ask it in his name. But Jesus will do it in his own way. At times we may not be aware of how he has answered our prayers. But there's no doubt that he will answer them, if his promises can be trusted.

But what can he mean when he says we will do "even greater works than these" (John 5:20)? At the time of Jesus' miracles, he had not yet died on the cross; the sacrifice for sin had not yet been accomplished, and the Holy Spirit had not yet been given. After he spoke those words, he accomplished those things, and then went back to the Father. As a result, Christians can now present the gospel to those who have not heard it. The message of salvation has since become clear: for those who now believe and accept Christ as their Savior, the Holy Spirit enters into and works in their lives. Jesus' amazing miracles did not accomplish this during his life on earth. In saying this, he looked ahead to what we would be able to do after his death and resurrection. Christians have been entrusted with a message through which they can lead people to salvation. Jesus looked ahead to what he would enable us to do, and proclaimed that these things were greater than the miracles he was performing.

The Church

As one becomes a Christian, one is not meant to live that life alone. As the gospel started spreading, local churches formed in every place where people came to believe. The book of Acts tells this story. That this is what God intended is clear from what he said about Adam at the very beginning: "It is not good for the man to be alone" (Genesis 2:18). It also arises naturally from the fact of the Trinity and what we have discussed previously; namely, that before God created anything, the greatest joy that the members of the Trinity must have known in their existence was the love that they shared with each other. Jesus made clear that this is exactly what he wanted for Christians when, on his last night before his crucifixion, he prayed:

> "My prayer is not for them alone. I pray also for those who will believe in me through their message, that all of them may be one, Father, just as you are in me and I am in you. May they also be in us so that the world may believe that you have sent me. I have given them the glory that you gave me, that they may be one as we are one—I in them and you in me—so that they may be brought to complete unity. Then the world will know that you sent me and have loved them even as you have loved me. (John 17:20-23)

Jesus did not intend that Christians live lives isolated from other Christians. He wanted Christians to live lives in which they experienced "complete unity" with other Christians, in the same way the members of the Trinity know it. Indeed, he taught that the unity that Christians would know together was to be a sign to the world of two things: first, that God the Father had sent the Son, and second, that the Father loved them as he loved the Son.

In this world, neither we, nor the church, are free from sin. Paul was brutally honest in his letters in the New Testament when he pointed out the serious flaws in the various churches he started. But despite their flaws, he never counseled Christians to stay away from the church or live private lives isolated from other believers.

Today, the flaws of modern churches are also evident. But nevertheless, Jesus' teaching stands:

> A new command I give you: Love one another. As I have loved you, so you must love one another. By this everyone will know that you are my disciples, if you love one another. (John 13:34-35)

If we decide that although we have become Christians we do not want to have anything to do with a local church, how are we to demonstrate that we are Christ's disciples? Rather, it is through showing love to broken individuals in flawed churches that we demonstrate how our lives have been transformed through Jesus' love.

True, not all churches that call themselves "Christian" accept the gospel; that is, not all accept the fact that we are sinners in need of a Savior. Many churches today look to Jesus only for moral teachings, and miss the critical point that we need him as our Savior. Additionally, not all churches that accept the basic truth of the gospel are concerned with showing the love to which Christ calls us. We may have to look for a local church that is both true to the gospel and that shows, however imperfectly, the love of Christ. And when we find it, we will not be alone anymore. The church is a setting in which Jesus wants us to know something of the joy that love brings to the members of the Trinity. Jesus wants us to know—through our relationship with the Father, with him, and with other Christians—something of the wonder of what lives that have this kind of love can be.

The Life God Offers

The many beneficial and positive aspects of the Christian life, as the Bible describes it, are, needless to say, more than can be considered here. There have been countless books that have been written regarding the Christian life over the last 2000 years. But for our purpose, enough has been said. The Christian life is a life worthy of a good and loving God.

CHAPTER 6

The Knowledge of the Truth about God

We have been considering the possibility that Christianity is true, and asking if it makes sense. The argument has been that Christianity does offer a sensible explanation of how a God of love is, through the events taking place in this world, going to achieve a wonderful goal: the creation of a new earth in which all who love God can live with the members of the Trinity forever. There is nothing irrational about the plan Christianity sets forth, and it is a plan worthy of a good and loving God.

One thing, however, the argument set forth in the preceding chapters cannot claim for itself is that it has established that Christianity is actually true. It is one thing for Christianity to make sense; it is another thing for it to be *true*.

Over the years, logical arguments have been made for the existence of God. Whether any of these arguments have succeeded, they have seemingly had a limited effect—such arguments do not appear to have resulted in large-scale conversions of the masses. And here we are concerned not only with the existence of God, but specifically with the truth of Christianity. No claim is here being made that its truth has been established. But given what the plan of Christianity is, one would not expect that arguments would conclusively establish its truth. God's concern is not to find smart people who can understand complex arguments. Rather, God is looking for people with contrite and repentant hearts who regret the selfishness and sinfulness of their lives. These are the people he can change into those who can live with him forever.

Those who come to be truly repentant for their sin will see that the story of Jesus dying for their sins fits their need perfectly. It is like Bilbo and the dwarves, in *The Hobbit*, needing to be in the right place at the right time to see the keyhole for the door into the mountain. Being spiritually in the right place lets one see, in Jesus' death on the cross, the solution to their problem. They will see something that those who have no concern for the selfishness and sinfulness of their lives will not see. A repentant person might wonder if it could really be true that Jesus died for their sins, but despite this questioning he or she will see that it meets their need. Seeing that it meets their need, they need only to pray to God, telling God that if it really is true, they want to accept it. When they have done this, they have become a Christian. And if Christianity speaks truth, then at this point, the Spirit of God enters into them. They have the Spirit of God *actually residing* in them. This presence of God's Spirit in them should confirm for them the truth of the Christian message.

This is not to say that doubts will not come. For some Christians, doubt remains a lifelong challenge. But for many if not most Christians, the presence of the Spirit in their lives will confirm for them the truth of their faith.

When Jesus returns, everyone will see that Christianity is true. But for now, the knowledge of its truth comes to those with repentant and contrite hearts who love Jesus, their Savior. This is exactly the type of plan that one would expect of a great God, a God who is best described as a God of love.

Acknowledgments

It was the classes I took with Dr. Alvin Plantinga at Calvin College that introduced me to the concept of different possible worlds, worlds that theoretically could have existed if, for example, we or God had decided to act in some way different than the way we actually acted. These classes led to the question that has stuck with me as to why God chose to create this world, instead of some other different world. Dr. Plantinga, then and now, has sought to show how Christian beliefs are neither illogical nor irrational. His example led me to believe that it was worthwhile to ponder such things as are addressed in this book.

The work of Francis Schaeffer also had an important early influence on me. He was a man who was convinced that Christianity answers the big questions of life. While I was in high school, I heard him lecture at the Presbyterian church I attended in Willow Grove, Pennsylvania. When I was a sophomore in college I spent six weeks at L'Abri

Fellowship, the community that he and his wife Edith started in Huemoz, Switzerland.

In contrast to the approach of many evangelical churches at the time—telling young people to just believe and not ask questions—here was place where all serious questions were taken seriously. It was full of visitors from many parts of the world and from many religious backgrounds—including atheists. It was exciting to see Christianity presented there, not as containing beliefs to be intellectually ashamed of, but rather as containing answers to the fundamental questions of life. I was a Christian before I went there, but the teachings I received there, and the experience of its loving, vital community, convinced me of the truth of Christianity in such a way that I have never since seriously doubted its truth.

While there I listened to tapes of a series of lectures that Francis Schaeffer had given some years earlier on the book of Romans. Since that time I have listened to these lectures again and again. A number of ideas set forth in this book flow directly from Schaeffer's teachings in those lectures. (The lectures are available for download at labri-ideas-library.org; an abbreviated version of these lectures can also be found in the book *The Finished Work of Christ* [Crossway, 1998].)

Acknowledgments

Also very helpful in my understanding of the book of Romans was a lengthy lecture series given by Dr. Martyn Lloyd-Jones in the 1950s and 1960s. These have been transcribed into a multi-volume set of books by Banner of Truth. (The lectures are also available for download at mljtrust.org.)

I would like to thank Tim Beals at Credo House Publishers for his assistance in bringing this project to fruition. I would also like to thank Mike Vander Klipp for his editorial assistance.

This book has been many years in the making. Many people have been kind enough to read and comment on various drafts of it, some of whom include: Themis Fotieo, Rev. Kevin Carr, Paul Lagrand, Dean VanBruggen, Sherri Rozema, Dane Vermerris, Arlene Warners, Alexandra Harper, Laura Mitchell, Gail Alt, Rev. Don Klop, David Kolbe, Ray Pater, and Steve Wykstra. I am grateful to them.

www.ingramcontent.com/pod-product-compliance
Lightning Source LLC
Chambersburg PA
CBHW060838050426
42453CB00008B/747